"The Hour Was One of Horror"

EAST CEMETERY HILL AT GETTYSBURG

"The Hour Was One of Horror"

EAST CEMETERY HILL AT GETTYSBURG

by
John M. Archer

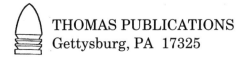

THOMAS PUBLICATIONS
Gettysburg, PA 17325

Cover design by Ryan C. Stouch

Cover illustration, "Night Assault," is courtesy of Dale Gallon

This book is dedicated to my parents,

Julian and Janet Archer,

who taught me to remember those who came before.

Photo Credits

A Note About the Maps

The original maps included with the text are the result of information gathered from the 1864 Bachelder Isometric Map, the 1869 Warren Survey Map, the 1876 Bachelder Maps and the turn-of-the-century maps produced under Col. E. Cope. Despite the extraordinary efforts of early surveyors to accurately depict the battlefield, these maps all contain inconsistencies and errors. Information from these maps has been combined with contemporary photographs and extensive field research to create the 1863 views presented here.

CONTENTS

The area of Menchey's Spring looking up hill toward the area defended by the 41st New York. The gatehouse is visible at the top of the hill.

ACKNOWLEDGEMENTS

I have been fortunate enough to have had the help of many generous and talented people in the preparation of this book. First and foremost, many thanks go to the staffs at the Bridgeport Historical Society and State Library in Connecticut, the Gettysburg National Military Park Library and the U.S. Army War College for their assistance in my research.

The cover illustration for this book appears courtesy of Dale Gallon. My gratitude goes to Mr. Gallon and the folks at his gallery, particularly Wayne Motts, whose enthusiasm for our history and its inhabitants is contagious. I am especially grateful to Beverly Bittle for giving her friendship, time and expertise in proofreading the manuscript. My appreciation to photographer Ron Karpin who donated his talents for many of the modern views. Thanks as well go to Warren Motts, Roger and Sue Height, Clyde James, and Trish Murphy who contributed materials and assistance to this work, and to Bill Clark, Mark Polley and all the other folks who were willing to lend an ear to my ideas or provide some moral support when necessary. My appreciation also to the folks at Thomas Publications for their help in seeing this book come to print. A special thanks goes to historian William A. Frassanito; his work on the changing appearance of the field at Gettysburg was an early inspiration for my research, and his expert advice since has aided in its completion.

Although the preparation of this book was a continual source of enjoyment for me, I was often less than a joy to be around. My greatest debt, then, is to the person who has always been there for me. Supportive of my projects from the first, my wife Darlene patiently put up with my frequent disappearances into the battlefield (whether I physically left the house or not), sympathized with my similarly frequent tirades about the quirks of computerdom, and on and on. Wife, I owe you.

PREFACE

It is a paradox of history that the significance of an event is often judged more by the attention it receives than by its inherent value. So it is with a historic site like the battlefield at Gettysburg. It is ironic then, but not surprising, that interest in one of the first areas chosen for preservation has declined dramatically.

Within days of the fighting in July 1863, the pivotal role of Gettysburg in the war was already apparent, and efforts were underway to preserve areas considered essential to commemorate the battle. In a letter written shortly after the armies left the field, Gettysburg lawyer David McConaughy stated:

> *[There is] no more fitting and expressive memorial of the heroic valor and signal triumphs of our Army...than the Battle-field itself, with its natural and artificial defences preserved and perpetuated in the exact form & condition they presented during the Battles.*
>
> *Acting at once on this idea I commenced negotiations on the most striking and interesting portions of the Battle ground, embracing among these the heights of Cemetery Hill on the centre, which resisted the fiercest assaults of the enemy, the Granite spur of Round Top on the left, with its massive rocks & wonderful stone defences...and the timber Breastworks on the right, extending for a mile upon the wooded heights of [Culp's] Hill, whose trees exhibit the fearful effect of our musketry fire.[1]*

Clearly the areas initially chosen for purchase, and certainly those most popular with early visitors, were where the scars of war intruded on the rural landscape. With its sweeping view of the town and battlefield from near the center of the Federal position, East Cemetery Hill was popular with early tourists and veterans' reunions alike. But as the scars faded and the historic significance and visual appeal of other areas became known, sites such as the High Water Mark, the Peach Orchard, and Devil's Den grew in popularity. In more recent years, media attention has drawn countless visitors to other areas of the field in search of motion picture scenarios and paranormal activity.

Today, the exigencies of development have permanently altered much of the ground around East Cemetery Hill, making it difficult to interpret the site and understand what made the area critical to the development of the battle. Equally frustrating is the fact that several modern histories of the battle give the struggle for East Cemetery Hill short shrift, or worse, are of questionable accuracy.

This study is an effort to remedy this oversight. It is not intended as a comprehensive history of the battle or the personalities of those who fought it. These areas have been admirably covered both in Edwin Coddington's *The Gettysburg Campaign—A Study in Command*, and Harry Pfanz's *Gettysburg—Culp's Hill and Cemetery Hill*. Nor is it my intention to overemphasize the importance of the fighting on East Cemetery Hill; the action in this area initiated more than its share of debate and "what if" scenarios. Instead, the reader is invited to tour this seldom explored segment of the battle, using first-hand accounts to help see the area—much of which has changed dramatically in the past 130 years—with a participant's eye. The text is accompanied by maps and photographs of the area that will help orient those on the field, as well as those unable to visit Gettysburg.

Some of the debates born of hindsight are unavoidable here; a few will be touched upon briefly in the context of the battle *as fought*. Others will no doubt occur to the reader. Indeed, some of the contemporary statements presented here contradict each other; one need only read a few Civil War accounts to realize that combatants rarely agreed in their interpretations of battle. I have attempted to suggest a setting that allows these disparate versions to exist side-by-side.

Whether in agreement or not, all the participants considered their part in the great battle as crucial to the final outcome. How history judges the significance of their acts is less important than remembering that all placed their lives on the balance to achieve that outcome.

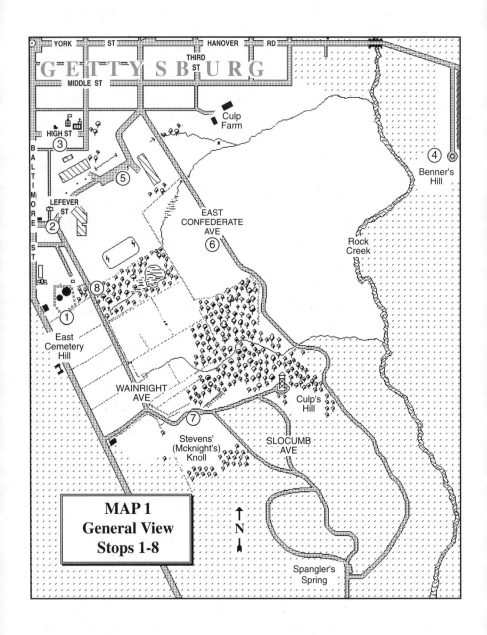

MAP 1
General View
Stops 1-8

N

JULY 1

"THE ONLY TENABLE GROUND..."

STOP 1 (Map 2)
Much as the Baltimore Pike divides Cemetery Hill at the edge of the borough, the fighting on the eastern part of the height developed a character distinct from that to the west. The text focuses on the area east of the road. Follow the Baltimore Pike (Rt. 97) to the Gettysburg Tour Center on East Cemetery Hill. Park in the visitor lot to the right (south side) of the Tour building. The following is a brief description of the first day's fight as it affected some of those who would occupy East Cemetery Hill.

When the rumble of artillery first reached Major General Oliver O. Howard and his staff south of Gettysburg, Union cavalry under Brigadier General John Buford had been engaged with advance elements of the Confederate army for some three hours. After placing his Eleventh Corps enroute from Emmitsburg at eight o'clock that morning, Howard rode ahead to rendezvous with Major General John Reynolds, commander of the Army of the Potomac's left wing. At about 10:30 a.m., however, as Howard neared Gettysburg, Reynolds was killed leading his First Corps in support of Buford's cavalry.

With the death of Reynolds, seniority placed Oliver Howard in command of all the Federal troops at Gettysburg. One of Howard's first—and most important—command decisions was to post his reserves on the broad height south of town known as Cemetery Hill.

> *After an examination of the general features of the country, I came to the conclusion that the only tenable position for my limited force was the ridge to the southeast of Gettysburg, now so well known as Cemetery Ridge. The highest point at the cemetery commanded every eminence within easy range.... I at once estab-*

1

lished my headquarters near the cemetery, and on the highest point north of the Baltimore pike.

Howard sent word to Major General Carl Schurz, now in command of the Eleventh Corps, to hurry on to Gettysburg. Receiving word that the right of the First Corps was being pressed, Howard proposed to place two of his divisions on Oak Hill, extending the Federal line northwest of Gettysburg; as a general reserve, Schurz' last division and three batteries were to remain on Cemetery Hill.[1]

Arriving with Barlow's First Division shortly after noon, Captain Michael Wiedrich's Battery I, 1st New York, was met on the Emmitsburg Road by one of Howard's aides and directed to East Cemetery Hill. Unlimbering their guns in

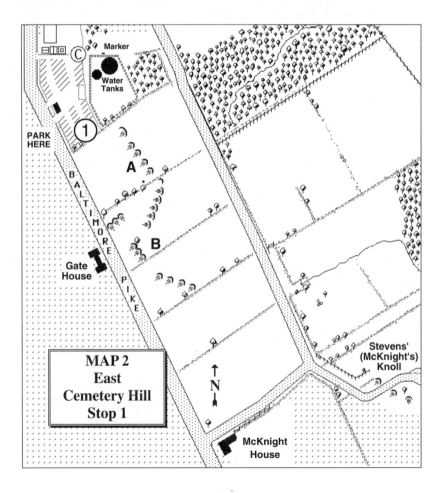

MAP 2
East
Cemetery Hill
Stop 1

East Cemetery Hill as it appeared near the turn of the century. (TC)

Turn-of-the-century view of Wainwright Avenue with iron gates.

the field northeast of the Cemetery gatehouse, Wiedrich's men were approached by Howard, who exhorted them to "hold this position at all hazards." As the rest of the Eleventh Corps streamed up the Taneytown Road, Howard pulled two more batteries out of column, Heckman's Battery K, 1st Ohio, and Wheeler's 13th New York Light, placing all ten guns in the field west of the gatehouse.[2]

Schurz pushed on through Gettysburg with his First and Third Divisions, and began to deploy in the fields north of the town. But the proposed link-up with Doubleday's First Corps stalled; arriving on Oak Hill first, and shortly after on the roads north of town, the advance elements of the Confederate Second Corps under Lieutenant General Richard Ewell moved into position around Schurz' two divisions.

In the meantime, the last of the Eleventh Corps had arrived: 2,861 men under Brigadier General Adolph von Steinwehr began to deploy around Cemetery Hill. Steinwehr reported: "I placed the First Brigade, Col. Charles R. Coster, on the northeast end of the hill, in support of Wiedrich's battery, which was then in position. The Second Brigade, Col. Orland Smith, took a position toward the northwest, supporting the reserve artillery of our corps."[3]

Despite repeated requests from Schurz for reinforcements, Howard was reluctant to commit more than Wheeler's battery from his reserves. Belatedly, and long after the tide of battle turned against the Federals, Coster's Brigade and Heckman's Battery were sent to Schurz, only to be given the daunting task of covering the Eleventh Corps' retreat. In the end, it seems Howard's energies to establish Cemetery Hill as a rallying point proved to be a mixed blessing. With his headquarters south of Gettysburg, Howard was far from the rapidly changing battle to the north and west—certainly too far to gauge the shaky condition of his two corps and withdraw them in a timely fashion. As Howard recalled:

> *About 4 p.m. I sent word to General Doubleday that if he could not hold out any longer, he must fall back, fighting, to Cemetery Hill and on the left of the*

4

Baltimore Pike; also a request to General Buford to make a show of force opposite the enemy's right, which he immediately did.... At 4:10 p.m., finding that I could hold out no longer, and that the troops were already giving way, I sent a positive order to the commanders of the First and Eleventh Corps to fall back gradually, disputing every inch of ground, and to form near my position....[4]

Regretfully, if Howard's orders contained any mention of routes for the withdrawal, word did not reach the rank and file. Unlike the Eleventh Corps, who passed Cemetery Hill to reach the field, First Corps units had gone directly into action through the fields southwest of Gettysburg. Lack of knowledge of the town and the new position added to the confusion of the retreat. By 4:15 p.m., the only major routes leading to Cemetery Hill—Washington Street and Baltimore Street—were choked with several thousand weary troops, batteries of artillery, ambulances, and sundry support vehicles of the two corps.

Pressing through the jumble of men and equipment in the west end of town was First Corps Artillery Chief Colonel Charles S. Wainwright. "There was very little order," Wainwright later wrote in his journal, "save that the Eleventh [Corps] took one side of the street and we the other; brigades and divisions were pretty well mixed up. Still the men were not panic stricken...." Wainwright had seen the last of his batteries off Seminary Ridge just ahead of the Gray battle lines, and now rode to the front of the column to establish a new position for his guns. "I rode on to the top of Cemetery Hill, the existence of which I now learned for the first time," Wainwright recalled. "Here I found General Howard, who expressed pleasure at seeing me, and desired that I take charge of all the artillery, and make the best disposition I could of it.... The General pointed out to me how he should form the two corps; stating that this spot must be held until the rest of the army came up." Leaving Wainwright to organize his artillery, Howard and his staff went about trying to get the badly disorganized infantry into position.[5]

Leave your vehicle now and walk to the artillery position across the wall (south) of the Tour Center parking lot (marked "A" on Map 2). Probably the first unit to be placed on East Cemetery Hill, Wiedrich's 1st New York Artillery, Battery B, was posted here by Howard at approximately noon on July 1. Note the up-ended gun tube on the right of Wiedrich's position, indicating the location of Howard's field headquarters. The vista from this spot was considerably more open in 1863, allowing Howard an unobstructed, albeit distant, view of much of the terrain surrounding the town. Upon reaching the hill, disorganized units of the Eleventh Corps reformed in the area behind the battery; the field here is probably the "lot" described in the following account.

At about the same time Wainwright rode through the west end of town, four skirmish companies of the 17th Connecticut under Major Allen Brady made their way into town from the east. Detached from Barlow's First Division earlier in the day, the group somehow managed to rejoin their regiment as

STOP 1—"I established my headquarters on the highest point north of the Baltimore Pike..." Howard's headquarters marker on East Cemetery Hill.

6

it withdrew through the town. Accompanied by Brigadier General Adelbert Ames, who now commanded the First Division for the fallen Barlow, the regiment then deployed in the street, "and poured destructive volleys into [the Confederate] ranks...but we found the enemy too many for us." Joining the retreat to Cemetery Hill, the regiment reformed their line near Wiedrich's guns, when Howard approached:

> About this time, Major-General Howard, who was in the thickest of the battle, regardless of danger, asked if he had troops brave enough to advance to a stone wall across a lot toward the town, and said he would lead them. We replied, "Yes, the Seventeenth Connecticut will," and advanced at once to the place indicated, remained a few moments, and again advanced across another lot still nearer the town and behind a rail fence....[6]

Jockeying an ambulance through the side streets and alleys of the town, Jacob Smith of the 107th Ohio wheeled up Baltimore Street to the bottom of Cemetery Hill.

> I saw a line of soldiers stationed on either side of the road, at right angles to the road, behind stone fences ready to repel the enemy. Then for the first time...I began to realize that our forces were...ready for another fray with the enemy. Many troops, no doubt, thought that it was an utter defeat of our forces and they made an effort to get as far away from the enemy as possible. It required a considerable effort on the part of our officers to get them into line and position again.[7]

One group, possibly part of the 107th Ohio under Colonel Seraphim Meyer, was less enthusiastic about rallying. "When the very first of the troops came up the pike there was a little reluctance manifested to face about, march back and form a new line of battle," Howard later wrote. "One colonel with a very straggling following of men, and having in his whole aspect a very wilted and drooping appearance, persisted in going eastward over the hill. [I] had sent an officer to turn him and his command back; seeing that he refused to obey, [I] promptly put him under arrest and put another officer in charge of the regiment. It was at this time, at about 4:30 p.m., that Major General Hancock came upon the field."[8]

Whether Howard would come to appreciate it or not, some much-needed assistance was arriving on Cemetery Hill. About midday, word had reached headquarters at Taneytown, Maryland, of Reynolds' death. Major General George G. Meade, commanding the Army of the Potomac, promptly dispatched Major General Winfield Scott Hancock to take command of the troops on the field, and determine if the situation warranted further concentration of the army.

As Hancock and his staff rode up the Taneytown Road, the remnants of two corps of the Army of the Potomac were in full retreat. Hancock's chief of staff, Lieutenant Colonel Charles Morgan, remembered, "No sound except scattering skirmish shots indicated that we were near the battle ground, but riding up on Cemetery Hill the whole field was before us." Near the Taneytown Road, Morgan could see officers of the 1st Corps attempting to reform their battered regiments. Buford's cavalry had taken position in the fields to the west, "as firm and immovable as if on parade. It was pleasant for the eye to look down from the confusion on the crest of the hill to the bold front presented by the cavalry below." Continuing east across the hill to the Baltimore Pike, Hancock was less impressed with Howard's efforts: "The rear of our troops was hurrying through town pursued by the Confederates. There had been some attempt to reform the Eleventh Corps as they passed over Cemetery Hill but it had not been very successful." Colonel Morgan agreed: "To what extent the 11th Corps had formed on the right and left of the Baltimore turnpike, I do not know, but I do know the road was literally full of men, many appearing to be organized regiments going to the rear. General Hancock and his staff rode in among them and by hard work succeeded in turning them into the field behind the stone wall."[9]

In the midst of the chaos, Hancock met with Howard near the Cemetery gate and informed him of Meade's instructions. Howard, no doubt surprised and insulted at the news of his replacement by a subordinate, decided "that was no time for talking," and to his credit, joined Hancock in continuing to forge a strong position on the hill.[10]

It is likely that both Howard and Hancock deserve more credit for stemming a Federal rout July 1 than each would later concede of the other. If Oliver Howard gave his men reason to stop on the heights, the appearance of Winfield Scott Hancock on Cemetery Hill gave the fought-out units reason to stay. Lieutenant Edward Whittier of the 5th Maine recounted, "I shall never forget, for I reported to him for orders, the inspiration of his commanding controlled presence, nor the fresh courage he imparted; his very atmosphere, strong and invigorating...." In the streets of the town below, there was no shortage of Southerners willing to test that resolve.[11]

On the heels of the retreating Federal units, Lee's jubilant Confederates swept into Gettysburg. Following the shattered Eleventh Corps into the north side of town were two brigades of Major General Jubal Early's Division. On the left of Early's line, Hoke's Brigade under Colonel Isaac E. Avery halted to reform along the railroad tracks on the north side of town. Taking advantage of the cover provided by the cut, the 6th, 21st, and 57th North Carolina regiments moved "400 yards to the left [east] and again moved forward." Skirting the buildings on the east edge of Gettysburg, the 1,200 Tarheels advanced south toward the William Culp farm off the Hanover Road. Still busy patching together a defensive line on East Cemetery Hill, Federal officers watched with concern. "A line of battle with skirmishers out was plainly seen east of town," recalled Colonel Morgan, "making its way towards Culp's Hill, and so far as I could see we had not even a skirmisher to meet it."[12]

Across the Baltimore Pike stands the entrance to Evergreen Cemetery and its distinctive brick gatehouse. Constructed seven years before the battle, the gatehouse stood prominently on the hilltop in 1863 and became the centerpiece for the new Federal line on the heights. Follow the path toward the gate and stop by the 4th Ohio monument (the white metal monument across the road from the gatehouse—marked as "B" on Map 2). Visible on the left just down the Pike is the frame and stone McKnight house mentioned in the following text, and up the Park road behind it, McKnight's Hill (now known as Stevens' Knoll). This knoll would come to play a key role in the defense of East Cemetery Hill.

The Evergreen Cemetery gatehouse as it appeared shortly after the battle. (TC)

"The only tenable position..." Photo looking north from the gatehouse shows the unobstructed view of the ground outside of Gettysburg in 1863. The wooden fence at the far side of the field marks the position of Harris' Ohio Brigade. (TC)

Not far from Morgan's position, Captain Greenleaf Stevens' 5th Maine, Battery E, pulled up near the cemetery gate to await orders. Spotting the six Napoleons, Hancock called out for the captain of "that brass battery." As described by Lieutenant Whittier:

> Captain Stevens heard what he said and put himself in Hancock's presence; he ordered Stevens to "take (his) battery on to that hill," pointing to Culp's Hill, and "stop the enemy from coming up that ravine." "By whose order?" was the inquiry. "General Hancock's," was the reply.

Separating his guns from the chaos atop the hill, Stevens led his battery east at the small farm lane just down the Pike, unlimbering his guns on the knoll behind the McKnight house. None too soon as it turned out, for Whittier could see Avery's Brigade advancing east of town. "As the battery reached this position the enemy was sweeping through the village and up across the lowlands in our front." Joined by Wiedrich's guns, the Maine battery opened fire on the gray lines. Unsupported by the rest of Early's Division, it is unlikely that Avery's small brigade could have gone much farther on their own, but the Federal gunners had made their point. "Shells from the enemy proving very effective," penned a North Carolina officer, "we were soon halted on the hillside, and the men ordered to lie down."[13]

To the west of Avery's line, Brigadier General Harry Hays reformed his brigade of 1,300 Louisiana "Tigers" in the town, pushing skirmish lines into the fields below Cemetery Hill to probe the new Federal line. A member of Company I of the 8th Louisiana, Lieutenant J. Warren Jackson recalled:

> The enemy was posted on Cemetery Hill about 600 yards from town & had command of every place near town or around it. Our position was a poor one and we were subjected to a galling fire from their sharpshooters—nobody [was] hurt—and we soon laid low in the grass, but their position was such a good one that they could see us...and I spent about 2 hours as miserably as I ever did in my life.[14]

11

Circa 1880 Tipton view looking south across East Cemetery Hill. The McKnight House is at far right; McKnight's Hill is on the left. One of the first markers on the battlefield, the original stone for Cooper's battery stands beside the tree at center.

By 5:30 p.m., Hancock and Howard had managed to post an impressive line of defense across the face of East Cemetery Hill. Positioned by Colonel Wainwright according to their firepower, five batteries frowned down from the heights between the cemetery gate and Culp's Hill alone. With their longer range, batteries of three-inch ordnance rifles were arrayed facing the open fields below the town: four of Wiedrich's guns still pointed north and east; across the wall on Wiedrich's right, another four rifled pieces of Captain James H. Cooper's 1st Pennsylvania, Battery B, faced east; and on Cooper's right, also facing generally east, were five rifles of Reynolds' 1st New York, Battery L, now commanded by Lieutenant George Breck. Behind Cooper's Battery, four of the larger-bored brass Napoleons of Lieutenant James Stewart's 4th U.S., Battery B, pointed up the Baltimore Pike in the event of a sudden attack from the town; located to the right on the saddle between Culp's Hill and Cemetery Hill, the six guns of Stevens' 5th Maine Battery could sweep all the ground to the north and east, particularly the fields just at the foot of the slope that Wainwright's other guns could not reach.

In support of the guns on the crest, Howard posted Ames' infantry division around the base of East Cemetery Hill. At the fence line on the northern slope of the hill was Ames' former brigade, now led by Colonel Andrew Harris, composed of the 17th Connecticut, and the 107th, 25th, and 75th Ohio regiments. Along the stone walls bordering the lane leading from a brickyard at the northeastern foot of the hill, Howard placed the 54th and 68th New York, and the 153rd Pennsylvania of Colonel Leopold von Gilsa's Brigade. Beyond von Gilsa's right, Hancock sent the remnants of Wadsworth's Iron Brigade of the First Corps to the far side of McKnight's Hill in support of Stevens' Battery.

As a member of Coster's 154th Pennsylvania remembered, "A line was formed...of every available man and everything done to make the enemy believe that we had a strong reserve force. He was either deceived or from some other cause he did not make any further advance that night." In one of the more controversial decisions of the battle, Ewell decided not to press the attack that evening. Besieged by doubts, not the least of which was the formidable appearance of the Federal line on Cemetery Hill, Ewell ordered his scattered corps to hold their positions. Justified or not, Richard Ewell had set the stage for the battle at Gettysburg that followed.[15]

Take a moment to walk around East Cemetery Hill and view the Federal position here. At the bottom of the eastern slope, the monuments marking the right of Ames' infantry line can be seen on Wainwright Avenue, originally known as Brickyard or Winebrenner's Lane. Ames' left was along the northern slope of the hill, where Harris' Brigade occupied a fenceline formerly located on the northern edge of the tour center lot.

No longer visible from Cemetery Hill, the positions eventually occupied by Early's Confederates are a short distance from the base of this hill. All of these positions will be examined in more detail later. Return to your vehicle for the following section.

As the Federal units reformed on the slopes of East Cemetery Hill, the extent of their losses struck home. Ames' Brigade had left Maryland that morning with about 1200 men. Including a 100 man detachment that arrived from Emmitsburg that evening, Colonel Harris was pained to find that the strength of his three Ohio regiments combined "did not exceed 500 men." The 17th Connecticut had arrived at Gettysburg with 386 men: "There was a detail of 100 men for picket from our regiment that night, but we were unable to furnish the full detail," recalled 2nd Lieutenant Albert Peck. "We were posted in an apple orchard close to the edge of the town, with our videttes posted along by a board and rail fence. We were ordered to be very watchful and vigilant...I don't think I got any sleep that night."[16]

Perhaps in light of the subsequent Northern victory at Gettysburg, veterans' accounts say little of the mood the night of July 1. But for many who had suffered yet another defeat by Lee's army, this time on Northern soil, the air of desperation must have been palpable: "Sad and solemn reflections possessed, at least, the writer of this paper," wrote one veteran from the Iron Brigade. "Our dead lay unburied and beyond our sight or reach. Our wounded were in the hands of the enemy. Our bravest and best were numbered with them...We had been driven, also, by the enemy and the shadow of defeat seemed to be hanging over us."[17]

July 2 — A.M.

"THE DREADFUL STRUGGLE BEFORE US..."

"This morning was fresh, balmy and pleasant," Jacob Smith of the 107th Ohio later recalled. "The sun shone mildly through an atmosphere still smoky from yesterday's conflict giving it the appearance of a huge ball of fire. All the world was quiet and at rest. There was nothing outside our immediate surroundings that would indicate...the dreadful struggle that was before us." That struggle was not long in starting.[1]

On picket in the orchard north of Harris' line, Lt. Peck of the 17th Connecticut observed, "As soon as it was light on the morning of the 2nd of July, we could see the Johnnies moving along the fences in our front, keeping out of sight as much as possible." From the cover of the yards and houses along Baltimore Street, the Southern skirmishers soon found the range:

It was not long before "zip" came the bullets from them, and our boys promptly returned their fire, although it was difficult to see them. Our boys took shelter behind the rail and board fences and apple trees, and once in a while the bullets would peel the bark from the trees, and there were a good many close shave.... [Sergeant] George Shaw, who was stationed behind an apple tree, and the Johnnies had got a range on him and were trying their best to sting him—their bullets cutting bark from the tree—but they did not hit him, and he was blazing away as fast as he could load and fire.[2]

As the morning wore on, the blue troops grew more resourceful at the push-and-shove sharpshooting match that had developed. The members of one Connecticut detachment came upon an effective method of dispatching their Southern counterparts:

We were all together under an apple tree, excepting one man who stood as outpost. We were annoyed very much by the frequent shots striking the ground around

15

us, and also the tree under which we were. No one was hit as yet, but we did not like to be shot at in that way and not know where it came from. Finally we discovered that the shots came from what appeared to be a hog-pen situated at the rear of a house about two or three hundred yards distant. ...So it was decided that four of our party should load and fire a volley into that hog-pen, and one of us reserve his fire to see the effect of the volley. As I was on the outpost, it was left for me to hold the reserve fire. As the smoke from the volley cleared away, three or four rebs were seen to clamber out of that hog-pen. Just as the last one was throwing his leg over the top board, I sent a "minnie" after him, and he went over sooner than he intended.[3]

Some of the combatants used less subtle methods. Deploying in the fields east of Cemetery Hill, the skirmish companies of von Gilsa's 153rd Pennsylvania under Lieutenant J. Clyde Miller came under a harrowing flank fire from the brickyard behind the McCreary house on Baltimore Street. Miller sent a runner to the heights behind him, and a few rounds from the Federal artillery sent the Southerners in search of safer ground.[4]

Silhouetted on the crest of Cemetery Hill, the Federal gunners themselves were conspicuous targets for the gray marksmen, and as the sun rose their losses mounted. In Wiedrich's Battery, sniper fire from a steeple in town had wounded two lieutenants and several others. "The gunner of the third piece, notwithstanding the orders not to fire into the town, loaded his gun with a shell and fired it at the steeple; it had the desired effect."[5]

The situation was scarcely better on the relatively sheltered crest of McKnight's Hill. Lt. Whittier of the 5th Maine recalled that, "Rebel sharpshooters had obtained a foothold in the corner of the fences and behind trees at various distances in front of the battery and...made it exceedingly dangerous to stand in any unprotected position on this extremity of Culp's Hill." While attempting to find the range of a group of the gray sharpshooters with a "French ordnance glass," Capt. Stevens himself was struck through both legs by a sharpshooter's bullet.[6]

By 2:00 p.m., the area between Cemetery Hill and the town had become a no-man's land. Still occupying the orchard, one of the 17th Connecticut recalled: "The Johnnies finally got a cross fire on us from the vicinity of the old tan yard [Rupp's tannery west of Baltimore Street] and it got so hot that we were finally relieved and moved back to our old position...." Returning to the rail fence, the New England regiment found that their brigade line had shifted, and they took position along a wall further east between the 25th and 75th Ohio.[7]

Most of the position held by the left of Ames' Division is sandwiched by private land, but can be seen from the Tour Center parking lot on the far side of the two water tanks. Carefully drive across the parking lot, paralleling the course of the chain-link fence at the back of the lot for about 100 yards to where it turns sharply to the right (marked "C" on Map 2). This east-west section of fence follows the course of part of the original "board fence" described in contemporary accounts, and marks the position of Harris' Brigade (a flank marker of the 107th Ohio is located about 40 yards down the fence). The orchard so fiercely defended by Lt. Peck's skirmishers extended roughly from where you are to the buildings north of the fence. As Lt. Jackson's Louisianans discovered, the Federal skirmishers in this area were able to fire "drop shots" on the gray line down the slope.

The shift of Harris' Brigade was one of several changes being taken to bolster the thin defensive line on East Cemetery Hill. The arrival of von Gilsa's 41st New York and the detachment of the 75th Ohio the previous night had added some 300 fresh troops, but General Ames' two brigades still numbered less than 1,300 men. Perhaps influenced by the fragile condition of his section of the line, as well as the heated skirmishing, Ames moved the 33rd Massachusetts of Smith's Brigade, 491 strong, across the Baltimore Pike in support of Wainwright's guns. The area behind the batteries was crowded with limbers and teams of horses, and the Massa-

STOP 1(c) – *Modern fenceline marking the position held by the Ohio Brigade. The left flank marker for the 107th Ohio stands in the brush along the fence.*

chusetts regiment fit in where they could: "One wing I placed in this turnpike," reported Col. Adin Underwood, "the other along the wall which runs nearly perpendicular to it." Nearby, above and behind Breck's Battery, Major Osborn had also placed six twenty-pound Parrott guns of Taft's 5th New York Light on the hillside west of the pike; four of these big guns now pointed toward the fields and high ground east of Cemetery Hill.[8]

Relieved of the sharpshooter's nest on their flank, the skirmishers of the 153rd Pennsylvania pushed out into the meadow southwest of the Culp farm. From the high ground of the meadow, Lt. Miller spied "quite a body of men in a depression of ground between us and the Rebel batteries on a hill behind them." If Miller sent word of his observation to his superiors—and he may well have—the information fell on deaf ears. Despite all the preparation on Cemetery Hill, misconceptions about the location and intentions of the Confederates almost spelled disaster for the Federals in the hours to come.[9]

STOP 2 (Map 3) ═══════════════════════════════════

Drive to the exit of the parking area and turn right, heading north on Baltimore Street. Drive just over .1 mile and turn right onto Lefever Street at the entrance to the Gettysburg schools. Carefully pull to the right curb for a moment. During the battle, the brick house on your left was owned by the Winebrenner family and stands on what was formerly the outskirts of Gettysburg. This home and a similar structure owned by the McCreary family located in the area to your right (since razed) served as shelter for Confederate marksmen. Bullet holes in the south side of this structure and the brick house across Baltimore street attest to the severity of their contest with the Federal skirmishers on the hill above. The brickyard occupied by the Confederate skirmishers in Lt. Miller's account was in the area to your right front. The northern end of Wainwright Avenue is to your right and generally follows the course of the old Brickyard (or Winebrenner's) Lane to the base of East Cemetery Hill.

Proceed up Lefever Street about 50 yards and turn into the alley on your left and stop. During the battle, a stream known as Winebrenner's Run ran across the low ground to your front and right. Now underground for most of its course, only the light colored concrete slabs and the storm drains running across the high school parking lot indicate the approximate course of the stream. This area is discussed in the following text.

═══

Among the skirmishers facing Lt. Miller that morning, J. W. Jackson and the skirmish companies of the 8th Louisiana still held their position below East Cemetery Hill. "Early on the morning of the 2nd we posted some advance skirmishers & placed the reserve behind a plank fence near town & there we had to stay—if anyone showed themselves or a hat was seen above the fence a volley was poured into us."[10] Only yards behind Jackson's men, two Confederate brigades lay unnoticed by the Federal command. Shortly before daylight, General Hays shifted his brigade of "Tigers"—the 5th, 6th, 7th, 8th, and 9th Louisiana regiments—out of Gettysburg into the fields northeast of Cemetery Hill. Taking advantage of the low ridge and knoll where Avery's Brigade halted the previous evening, Hays placed

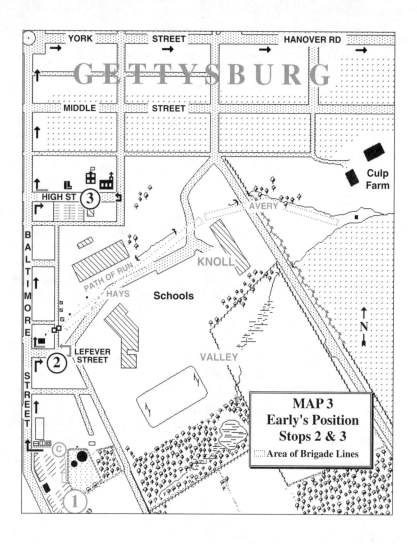

MAP 3
Early's Position
Stops 2 & 3
Area of Brigade Lines

his men on the right of the North Carolinians. The Confederate line now stretched along the small stream near the Winebrenner home on Baltimore Street to the Culp farm, some 800 yards to the northeast.[11]

As the day brightened, the view of the Federal position gave the Confederate command pause for thought. In his journal, Hays' adjutant, Capt. William Seymour, described their dilemma:

> *All night long the Federals were heard chopping away and working like beavers, and when*

STOP 2 – The Winebrenner house on Lefever Street.

the day dawned, [Cemetery Hill] was found to be crowned with strongly built fortifications, and bristling with a most formidable array of cannon. Gen. Ewell, in sending us to this advanced position, intended forming his general line of battle upon us, but when daylight came, he discovered it was impracticable to do so. He expressed great anxiety to withdraw our brigade, but this could not be done without immense loss in face of the powerful batteries on the hill which could sweep...the field over which we would have to pass in retiring.[12]

East of Baltimore Street, the right of Hays' line found themselves pinned to the bank of Winebrenner's Run. "We had to remain there...hugging the ground behind a very low ridge which only partially covered us from the enemy's fire," Capt. Seymour wrote. "It was almost certain death for a man to stand upright." Before sundown, forty-five of the Louisianans would fall to the Federal skirmish fire alone.

STOP 3 (Map 3) ══════════════════════════

Return to the intersection with Baltimore Street and turn right, heading north. Identified by small metal plaques, many of the homes you see on either side of the street were here at the time of the battle. Proceed .2 mile to High Street and turn right. To the left, note the large brick building that housed the public school and beside it, the former German Reformed Church. Both structures served as hospitals and appear in the following accounts. There is no parking on the right side, so on reaching Stratton Street turn around and park on the other side of High Street. You may wish to walk to the rear of the lot across from the school building to view the ground between High Street and the Union position (the water tank serves as a reference point for the location of the crest of East Cemetery Hill). Try to envision the open fields that existed at the time of the battle between here and the Union position (the area's 1863 appearance is shown on Map 6). Return to your vehicle for the following section.

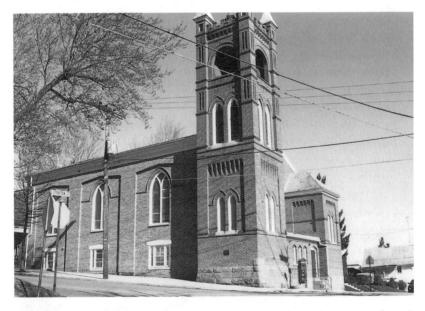

STOP 3 – *The former German Reformed Church on the corner of High and Stratton Streets served as a hospital for Eleventh Corps prisoners.* (RK)

The old school building on High Street. The "gabled" house mentioned in the text is to the left.

By the morning of July 2, several of the larger structures in town had been pressed into service as hospitals for those injured in the previous day's battle. Ironically, while Hays' skirmishers battled it out with Howard's men on the morning of July 2, many of the wounded prisoners from the Eleventh Corps were brought to the public school and the German Reformed Church on High Street—just behind Hays' position.

Taken prisoner after being wounded on July 1, Private Justus Silliman of the 17th Connecticut had a unique view from one of the public school windows: "We are in full view of the battlefield, the Confederate line of battle being within a few rods in front of our hospital. Our own line is also in full view. They occupy a line of hills which they have fortified." Concealed in the low ground southeast of the old school, Hays' line lay "stretched on the ground under cover of a low ridge and spent the afternoon in eating, sleeping and card playing."[13]

The private homes on High Street also provided a convenient roost for Southern sharpshooters. While a prisoner in the church, Private Reuben Ruch of the 153rd Pennsylvania watched one unlucky marksman at his work:

> *I saw one get on the roof of a two story house. He was firing over the chimney, and I thought it a bad position. If he were to get hit and stunned, the fall would kill him. He had fired four rounds and was getting ready for another, and in the act of looking over the chimney was hit and fell off the gable end. After the battle I looked up the fellow to see where he was hit, and found that the ball had pierced his forehead.[14]*

Before leaving this stop, note the two-story brick house beyond the church and next to the old public school; this may well have been the gabled building described by Private Ruch in his account of the Confederate sharpshooter. Stay with your vehicle for the following section.

"It was...a comforting thought that Lee, who, as rumor had it, had wished and hoped for a defensive battle," Gen. Schurz later wrote, "was now obliged to fight an aggressive one against our army established in a strong position." Lee's plans for July 2 were aggressive indeed. They called for Lieutenant General James Longstreet to swing his First Corps around to the south and attack the Union left flank end on, supported by successive attacks from A. P. Hill's Third Corps as the battle rolled north. At the same time, Ewell was to make a "diversion" on the Union right with Early's and Major General Edward Johnson's Divisions, "to be converted to a real attack if an opportunity offered."[15]

Lying in the stifling heat on the low ground southeast of town, Early's Louisiana and North Carolina regiments would have a long wait under a "withering" sun before receiving their orders for the attack. After a series of delays, it was almost 4:00 p.m. before Longstreet was even in position to begin his assault.

24

STOP 4 (Map 4)

Drive back up High Street to Baltimore Street. Turn right at the light and proceed to the town square, where you will again turn right onto York Street (Route 30 East). Drive .3 mile and at the fork in the road, drive straight onto Route 116 (Hanover Road). About .4 mile on your left, you will see the upturned gun tube marking the location of Ewell's headquarters on July 2. Proceed another .4 mile and turn right at the sign for Benner's Hill. Follow the Park road to the end and turn around. Stop in a spot where you will not block the road.

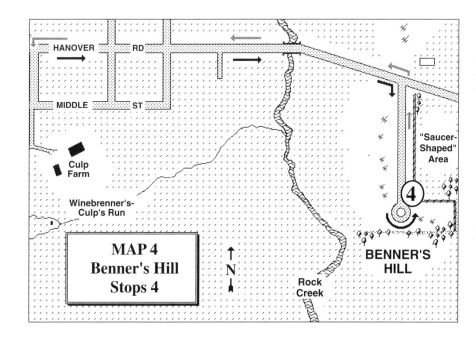

BENNER'S HILL

"A MIGHTY STORM OF IRON HAIL..."

Any decision by Richard Ewell concerning an attack would rely heavily on the success of his Second Corps artillery in neutralizing the Federal guns on East Cemetery Hill. Strangely, of the eighty-odd guns available to him, Ewell decided to use only thirty-two pieces to bombard the Federal position. On the morning of July 2, three batteries of Dance's Battalion took position behind Ewell's right near the Seminary buildings, extending the long line of batteries supporting Longstreet on Seminary Ridge. But the principal responsibility for the bombardment rested on the shoulders of a nineteen-year-old former V. M. I. student, Major Joseph W. Latimer. Commanding Johnson's divisional artillery in place of the wounded Lieutenant Colonel R. Snowden Andrews, the young major was a favorite of the Southern officer corps for his dedication and skill.

Latimer had spent the early morning hours of July 2 searching east of Gettysburg for an artillery platform for his

STOP 4 – View to the west from Latimer's guns on Benner's Hill. The gatehouse on Cemetery Hill is visible just above the plaque in the foreground. (RK)

four batteries, eventually settling on Benner's Hill, a broad, wheat-covered height on the Hanover Road. For most of the afternoon of July 2, Latimer kept his Battalion under cover. Although the Federal right was an easy target some 1400 yards to the southwest, Latimer was no doubt aware that, conversely, Wainwright's artillery also commanded the open crest of Benner's Hill.[1]

Between 4:00 and 5:00 p.m., the rumble of Longstreet's artillery announced the assault on the Union left, and Latimer's four batteries raced up the slope and unlimbered. Along the crest south of the Hanover Road, Latimer placed his smaller guns—a mixture of smoothbore Napoleons, rifled Parrott guns and Ordnance pieces—fourteen guns in all. On the knoll just to the north of the road, Latimer placed his pair of heavier twenty-pound Parrott guns joining Graham's Virginia Battery of four heavy guns sent earlier from Dance's Battalion.

On July 2, 1863, Confederate guns lined the hilltop from behind your position to the knoll on the other side of the Hanover Road. Leave your vehicle and walk along the line of guns to the marker for Dement's 1st Maryland Battery. Looking back to the west, locate the aqua-colored water tanks on East Cemetery Hill. Between the tanks and the National Tower to the left, you may be able to see the cemetery gatehouse marking the center of Wainwright's artillery line. Beyond the treeline on your left, a smaller observation tower marks the top of Culp's Hill.

From Seminary Ridge to the west of Gettysburg, and Benner's Hill to the east, a converging fire arched into the Federal positions across the face of Cemetery Hill. "The shots came thick and fast," one veteran recalled, "bursting, crushing and ploughing, a mighty storm of iron hail, a most determined and terrible effort of the enemy to cripple and destroy the guns upon the hill." Pvt. Silliman of the 17th Connecticut remembered: "The cannonading and musketry firing was terrific and the sound of shells rushing through the air was continuous and resembled somewhat that of a tremendous waterfall."[2]

East Cemetery Hill was well within the range of Dance's guns near the Seminary, but it was the well-aimed shots screaming in from Latimer's batteries that began to tell on Wainwright's guns. At the center of the position, Cooper's and Breck's gunners caught the brunt of the barrage. One twenty-pound shell exploded directly under Cooper's left gun, managing to kill or wound all five men working the piece, but leaving the weapon intact. Before their fallen comrades were cleared from the scene, a new gun crew sent a shot in reply. Another well-placed hit cracked the axle of another of Cooper's rifles; undaunted, its crew continued firing the piece until the gun finally collapsed. Nearby, one of Breck's rifles was also struck on the axle and disabled. Just to the rear of the guns, another hit sent one of the New Yorkers' caissons up with a roar.[3]

While Wainwright observed the fire of Wiedrich's Battery, a shell burrowed into the ground at his feet: "I waited quietly to see if it would drive out the hole it entered when it burst, or would it break out straight up. It never occurred to me that should it come right up it would certainly hit me, until it had safely blown out its entrance." "I realized afterwards how indifferent one becomes to the danger when you are accustomed to the flying around of cannon balls, even to feeling they are harmless...."[4]

Posted behind Wainwright's batteries, the 33rd Massachusetts was caught in the crossfire from the two ridges. Colonel Underwood later wrote: "[We] were very much exposed to the enemy's severe fire, the wing along the wall so much so, and the shot and shell came from so many different directions, that...I changed its position from one side of the wall to the other, two or three times." Attempting to confer with Ames at the wall across from the Cemetery gatehouse, Wainwright witnessed another twenty-pound shot plow into a line of infantry, probably that of the Massachusetts regiment. "Taking the line sideways, it literally ploughed up two or three yards of men," Wainwright recalled, "killing or wounding a dozen or more. Fortunately, the shot did not burst, for it struck so near where we were sitting that it covered us with dust." Small wonder that Wainwright found Latimer's fire to be "the most accurate I have ever seen on the part of their artillery."[5]

Although the bombardment wrought havoc in the batteries on the crest of Cemetery Hill, Ames' infantry just down the slope was relatively unscathed: "We hugged the ground pretty close, and some of the shells burst over our heads," Lt. Peck wrote, "but I do not remember that any of our brigade were either killed or wounded, although we were very much exposed. I do not think we should have gotten off so well if we had been under fire of our own batteries so long."[6]

Indeed, for on Benner's Hill, Major Latimer's fears about the nature of his position were confirmed. The Southern guns had no sooner opened, when Federal counter-battery fire began to sail into his exposed position. Joined by sections of Twelfth Corps artillery (Atwell's Pennsylvania Battery and Kinzie's 5th United States) on the narrow crest of Culp's Hill, Wainwright's guns pounded the Southern position. "At once, as if directed by the command of one man, our battery united with Battery L, 1st N.Y., Lieut. Breck, with Cooper and Wiedrich on the hill, and with Taft's twenty-pounders in the Cemetery, and poured such destructive fire onto the batteries on Benner's Hill," wrote Lt. Whittier, "four of their limbers or caissons exploded and their batteries were silenced." Midway down Latimer's line, Carpenter's Allegheny Battery was particularly hard hit, losing almost a third of its ninety-one members and nine horses. Near the Hanover Road, Capt. William Brown of the Chesapeake Artillery had also been badly wounded, one of his Parrott guns disabled, and only two of the remaining pieces still able to maintain fire.[7]

Return to your vehicle and proceed a few yards back up the Park road. When traffic allows, stop by the marker for Brown's guns and walk to the fenceline on the east side of the hill and note the low ground beyond. During the battle, this now quiet slope was lined with the limbers, caissons, and teams of horses belonging to Latimer's guns. This hillside is the same described in the account that follows (see Map 4).

The uneven contest continued for almost two hours before Latimer requested to be withdrawn from his position. Passing the hillside, Adjutant Robert Stiles was stunned by the damage to Latimer's batteries:

> [The battalion] had been hurled backward, as it were by the very weight and impact of the metal from the position it had occupied on the crest of the ridge into the saucer-shaped depression behind it; and such a scene as it presented-guns dismounted and disabled, carriages splintered and crushed, ammunition chests exploded, limbers upset, wounded horses plunging and kicking, dashing out the brains of men tangled in the harness....[8]

In all, Latimer's Battalion lost fifty-one men and thirty horses to the fire of the Federal gunners. With Major General Johnson's permission, Latimer withdrew his artillery, leav-

*"The Battalion had been hurled backward into a saucer-shaped depression..."
Modern photo looking northeast across the reverse slope of Benner's Hill. (RK)*

ing two of Dement's Napoleons and Raine's two rifles to support the attack on the Federal right. Minutes later, the advance of Johnson's Division toward Culp's Hill again drew attention to Latimer's guns. Again the Federal gunners opened on Benner's Hill and silenced the Southern guns, this time mortally wounding the young major in the exchange.[9]

STOP 5 (Map 5; Map 6 for 1863 appearance) ═══════════
Return to the intersection with the Hanover Road and turn left. Go .6 mile and turn left onto Third Street. At the stop sign at East Middle Street, note the William Culp farm to your left front. Now maintained by the National Park Service, the Culp farm marked the left of Early's line on July 2. As a reference, the west slope of Benner's Hill is visible on your left beyond the Culp barn.

Turn right onto East Middle Street, drive one block to the stop sign at Liberty Street, and turn left. Bear to the right, entering the school area on Lefever Street and drive .1 mile. Bear to the right past the entrance to the elementary school and pull into parking area on your left.

Although the terrain around you was dramatically altered with the school construction, the knoll and low ridge mentioned in Southern accounts are still evident here (see Map 6). Concealed by the rise of ground in front of you, the Confederate line generally followed the course of Winebrenner's Run, which can be seen as it reappears in the depression to your left rear. On the hill behind you is the former German Reformed Church, from which Pvt. Ruch watched Hays' Louisianans on July 2. In 1863, the fields between here and Cemetery Hill were marked only by wooden fencelines. You may stay in your vehicle for the following section.

EARLY'S ADVANCE

"*EVERY GUN WAS BROUGHT TO BEAR...*"

From Richard Ewell's perspective, there was still time to turn the "diversion" into a full scale assault and he issued instructions to his division commanders. As Jubal Early reported:

> *The fire from the artillery having opened on the right and left at 4 o'clock, and continued for some time, I was ordered by General Ewell to advance upon Cemetery Hill with my two brigades that were in position as soon as [Major] General [Edward] Johnson's division, which was on my left, should become engaged at the wooded hill on the left, which it was about to attack, information being given to me that the advance would be general, and made also by Rodes' division and Hill's division on my right.*
>
> *Accordingly, as soon as Johnson became warmly engaged, which was a little before dusk, I ordered Hays and Avery to advance and carry the heights in front.*[1]

"Just before dark the solitary figure of old Gen. Early is seen emerging from the streets of the town," Capt. Seymour of Hays' staff recalled, "and riding slowly across the field in the direction of our position; the little puffs of dust that rise from around his horse's feet, show that the Federal sharpshooters are paying him the compliment of their special attention." "A little before 8 p.m.," recalled Gen. Hays, "I was ordered to advance with my own and Hoke's brigade on my left, which had been placed for a time under my command." Captive Justus Silliman could see Hays' brigade line forming near his hospital: "Just at dusk we saw those infallible L[ouisian]a Tigers make preparations for a charge. They stealthily formed in line under cover of a hill and slowly and in excellent order advanced toward our lines...."[2]

To the left of the Louisianans, Colonel Isaac Avery's Tarheels formed their battle line in the low ground near the Culp farm. On the right of the brigade line, the 6th North Carolina unfurled their prized regimental flag, "a silken banner...embroidered

[with] the coat of arms of North Carolina." Waiting with the 21st North Carolina in the middle of the brigade, Major James Beall later recalled, "After lying all day under a July sun, suffering with intense heat, and continually annoyed by the enemy's sharpshooters from the heights, from sheer desperation, we hailed with delight the order to again meet the veteran foe."[3]

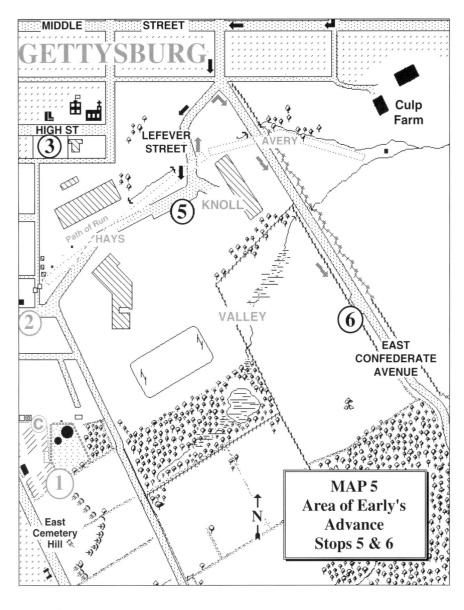

MAP 5
Area of Early's
Advance
Stops 5 & 6

STOP 5 – *"The line was formed along a little rivulet..."* View to the southwest across the remaining section of Winebrenner's Run. The Southern line was sheltered by the low ridgeline at the photo's center. Although this area was open farmland in 1863, only part of East Cemetery Hill is visible today between the tower and the school building. (RK)

North slope of the "knoll" occupied by Hays' men, and the former German Reformed Church on the hill beyond. In 1863, the Confederate line here was in clear view of Federal prisoners in the church.

The 57th North Carolina formed the far left of the Southern line. Colonel Hamilton Jones remembered: "The sun was low when the order came, and when the bugle sounded the advance, the line advanced in beautiful order, and as it pointed to the southwest there was a glint all along the line of bayonets that was very striking and marked how beautifully they were aligned." In a letter to his brother just weeks after the battle, Lt. J. W. Jackson of Hays' 8th Louisiana was less enthusiastic: "I felt as if my doom was sealed—and it was with great reluctance that I started my skirmishers forward."[4]

Across the meadows on McKnight's Hill, Lt. Whittier, now in command of the 5th Maine, supervised the refitting of the battery after the duel with Latimer's Battalion. At Wainwright's suggestion, Whittier's crews stocked the limbers of each piece, and the empty caissons were sent to the rear for refilling. Whittier later recalled:

It was about 7:30 to 7:45 p.m.; the sun had dropped behind the Cumberland mountains, and the dusk of evening was creeping through the valley of Rock Creek, when we made out the lines of the enemy at a distance of 1,000 yards, forming near the house and farm buildings of William Culp, on the outskirts of town.

"Up went the lids of the limber-chests, the fuses were cut in another moment, and the guns were loaded as if on drill." Using distances plotted that afternoon with Stevens' "French ordnance glass," the smoothbores opened on Hays' battle lines with uncanny accuracy. "As quickly as the enemy appeared, even while his lines were forming, the battery opened with case-shot, each one bursting as if on measured ground, at the right time and in the right place in front of the advancing lines."[5]

Watching the advance from the German Reformed Church behind the gray battle line, Pvt. Ruch of the 153rd Pennsylvania described the grim harvest:

Between the Rebel and Union positions was a ridge about six or eight feet high. The Johnnies started stooped over, scattered like a drove of sheep, till they got to this ridge. Then every man took his place, and giving the Rebel yell; by this time our grape and canister began to plow gaps through their ranks. They closed up like water, and advanced on the double quick. This was a very interesting sight for me, for I was sitting back and looking on...no one can see much of a fight while he is in it. To see grape and canister cut gaps through the ranks looks rough. I could see heads, arms, and legs flying amidst the dust and smoke...it reminded me much of a wagon load of pumpkins drawn up a hill, and the end gate coming out, and the pumpkins rolling and bounding down the hill.[6]

In spite of the carnage, Hays' battle line, close to 2,500 strong, cleared the first ridge, descending into a low area of land that gave the Southerners some respite from the Federal guns. "[We] are down in the valley in a trice," recalled Capt. Seymour, "the Yankee missiles are hissing, screaming and hurtling over our heads, but doing very little damage."[7]

STOP 6 (Map 5; Map 6 for 1863 appearance) ━━━━━
Backtrack up the school road .1 mile and turn right onto East Confederate Avenue. As you proceed up this road, note that Winebrenner's Run (more accurately called Culp's Run in this area) runs under the road here and passes to your left behind the Culp buildings. The knoll on your right and the low ground along the run sheltered Avery's men while they waited to attack Cemetery Hill. Partially covered today by the school stadium, the "valley" described by Capt. Seymour is the low area to your right just past the elementary school. At the top of the rise, stop in the turnout on the right.

Advancing up the next slope, the left of Hays' line began driving the Federal skirmishers from Culp's Meadow. "Towards sundown their skirmishers appeared followed by two lines of battle in the rear," wrote Lt. Miller of the 153rd Pennsylvania. "We now commenced falling back: I remember halting [my men] three times and firing." It was then the Pennsylvanians' turn to double-quick, and Miller and his men retired southward to clear a field of fire for the Federal line at Brickyard Lane.[8]

36

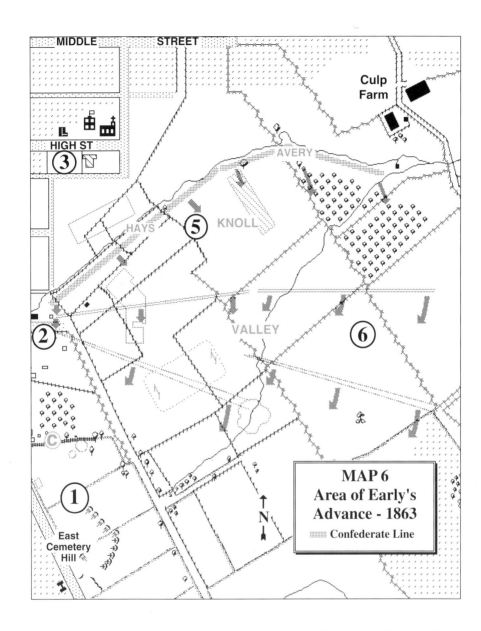

As the Union skirmish lines withdrew, Captains Wiedrich, Ricketts and Breck ordered their gunners to open, and the fifteen guns sent a torrent of metal toward the Confederate lines. "His sharpshooters emptied their rifles at us and fell back to their main line at once," recalled Capt. Neill Ray of Avery's 6th North Carolina, "and every gun was brought to bear on us. The fire was terrific, but our men moved forward very rapidly, bearing to the right, having the batteries on Cemetery Hill as their objective point."[9]

In 1863, this area was the edge of the orchard that extended northward to the Culp buildings. Then as now, the area beyond the fence on your right was largely open. Much of the difficulty in interpreting the action in this area arises from the modern treelines that obscure the view of the Federal position. The Federal batteries described in the preceding account were located to the left of the water tank visible beyond the trees across the field. Further to the left, Stevens' 5th Maine Battery was located on the saddle just behind the treeline extending from Culp's Hill. Crossing the high ground around you, the Southern ranks were exposed to a converging fire from both locations.

Shortly after the start of the advance, Early's brigades began a maneuver designed to swing the left of the long Southern line to the west to strike the Union positions at the base of Cemetery Hill. "As soon as the summit of the hill was gained, it was discovered that the batteries we had been ordered to take were in front of Hays' brigade, and considerably to the right of our right flank," wrote Colonel A. C. Godwin, "Colonel Avery now ordered a change of front and succeeded in wheeling the brigade to the right, a movement which none but the steadiest veterans could have executed under the circumstances."[10]

Yet the maneuver—pivoting 2,500 men over broken ground while under heavy fire—was apparently routine enough to the participants to receive little other mention in Southern reports. General Hays' report does not mention this, but it is likely that most of his brigade also needed to realign during the advance. On the outside of the turn, Avery's three North Carolina regiments had substantially more ground to cover. For the maneuver to succeed, Avery's men may well have started their advance first, forming the second line described by Federal observers, perhaps just ahead and to the left of

STOP 6 – *"The Yankee missiles are screaming, hurtling over our heads..."* Looking southwest across the "valley" mentioned in Southern accounts. Stevens' Knoll is behind the modern treeline at left; East Cemetery Hill is to the right. Col. Avery is said to have fallen in the area to the right. *(RK)*

"We descended into a low bottom..." Modern view looking south across the ground described by Col. Godwin. Advancing from left to right here, the North Carolinians were exposed to flank fire from Steven's Knoll *(left center)*.

the Louisiana troops. Viewed from the 5th Maine's position on McKnight's Hill, the sight was unforgettable: "When the enemy started on this movement their lines nearly faced our position, but as they advanced they obeyed the order given at the outset, and, pivoting on their right which rested on and moved along the outskirts of the town, they...changed direction by an almost right half-wheel of their whole force...."[11]

One of the few mounted figures in the advance, Avery rode at the right of his line near the juncture of the two pivoting brigades. Advancing with his old regiment, the 6th North Carolina, Avery was struck in the neck with a musket ball, and fell mortally wounded half-way to his objective. Unaware of their loss in the fading light and billowing smoke, Avery's men completed their wheel and pushed on toward the Union position.[12]

STOP 7 (Map 7; Map 8 for 1863 appearance) ===============
Return to your car and continue up the Park road. The road here follows the contours of the base of Culp's Hill, the target of the attack by Johnson's Division shortly before Early's advance. The Confederate line crossed from the woods on your left up the slopes to the right.

At the stop sign at Spangler's Spring (about 1 mile), turn right and then bear right, following the Union position along the crest of Culp's Hill. Drive .6 mile to the next stop sign, turn left. Proceed .1 mile and park in the turnout on McKnight's Hill (known today as Stevens' Knoll).

The position of the 5th Maine is clearly visible on the hillside to your left and front. The goal of Early's attack, the Federal position on East Cemetery Hill, is to your right front. The rolling fields to your right have changed little since 1863. Although modern treelines have changed some of the vista, the field of fire available to Stevens' gunners as the Southerners wheeled across their front is still evident. As a reference, the modern buildings visible several hundred yards beyond the treeline are located near the Culp Farm and just behind the Confederate position. Note the breastworks running up the slope in the trees behind you. These traces mark the left of the support position taken by the Iron Brigade on the evening of July 1. Stay in this area for the next section of text.

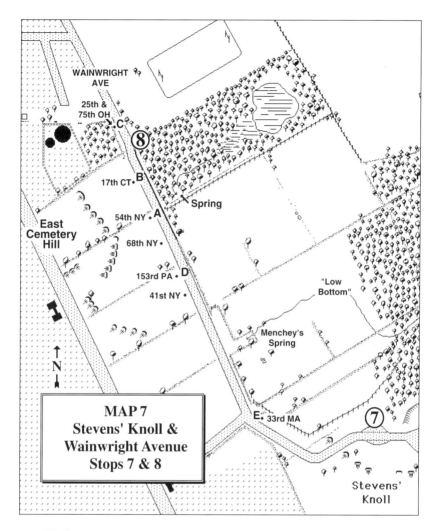

WAINWRIGHT AVE

25th & 75th OH

C

(8)

17th CT • B

Spring

54th NY • A

East Cemetery Hill

68th NY •

153rd PA • D

41st NY •

"Low Bottom"

Menchey's Spring

N

MAP 7
Stevens' Knoll &
Wainwright Avenue
Stops 7 & 8

E • 33rd MA

(7)

Stevens' Knoll

Within minutes of Latimer's cannonade, confusion about the Southern intentions began to tell on East Cemetery Hill. After firing almost five hundred rounds of ammunition that afternoon, Cooper's four guns were withdrawn from East Cemetery Hill, relieved by the six rifled pieces of the 1st Pennsylvania Light, Battery F and G, commanded by Captain R. Bruce Ricketts. According to Ricketts, he was soon approached by both Ames and Wainwright, who warned him "that there would probably be a charge on that point, and Col. Wainwright said, 'Captain, this is the key to our position on Cemetery Hill, and must be held and in case you are charged

41

STOP 7 – *Looking north from Stevens' Knoll today. The Confederate position was in front of the modern buildings in the distance. Wainwright Avenue is visible on the left. (RK)*

here, you will not limber up under any circumstances, but fight your battery as long as you can.'"[13]

But with Early's two brigades hidden only 600 yards away, it was the advance of Johnson's 4,000 man division across Benner's Hill that gained the attention of the Federals. Unaware of the real threat to his line, Ames began shifting some of his regiments to the eastern slope. The recently arrived 41st New York under Lieutenant Colonel D. von Einsiedel, and Smith's 33rd Massachusetts had already been moved from their positions on the hill and deployed in the meadows to the east. Perhaps to make up for the departure of the 41st New York, Ames then ordered Harris to send the 17th Connecticut to support von Gilsa's Brigade at Brickyard Lane.[14]

[Note: The following is a short walking tour tracing the Eleventh Corps position around the base of the hill. If you wish to drive the route instead, follow the directions about .2 mile to the dirt turnout by the Ohio monument (marked as Stop 8 on Map 7). The walking tour will reach this area shortly.]

BRICKYARD LANE

"SURRENDER YOU DAMN YANKEES..."

Leave your vehicle in the turnout and proceed on foot along the Park road. At the base of Stevens' Knoll, bear to the right onto Wainwright Avenue. In 1863, the stone wall to your right became a convenient breastwork for the Federal troops along the lane. A few yards further up Wainwright Avenue, the parallel walls running down the hill on your right mark the location of Menchey's Spring, one of two springs where Federals risked the fire of Southern marksmen to obtain fresh water during the battle.

Just past the spring, note the grassy area just beside the road and the wooden gate beyond; these mark the original path of Brickyard Lane as it left the area of the spring and continued toward town along the far side of the remaining wall. (See Map 8. In 1863, stone walls bordered both sides of the original lane on this side of the modern gate. The missing section was probably removed when Wainwright Avenue was built in the 1890s). The monuments beyond the gate indicate the approximate position of the regiments of von Gilsa's Brigade.[1]

Proceed to the rise in the avenue and stop by the 54th New York monument (marked "A" on Maps 7 and 8). Across the road, a fenced farm lane ran to the northeast from the original Brickyard Lane. Traces of this path and another freshwater spring are still evident along the modern fenceline on the southeast edge of the woodlot.

Continue up the road to the area of the 17th Connecticut monument (marked "B" on Maps 7 and 8). The small trees and scrub brush that originally grew along the original lane here have been supplanted by the modern wood lot across the road. As you read the following text, remember that the view to the north and east was largely open in 1863.

Wainwright Avenue. The original path of Brickyard Lane followed the wall at the right through the modern gate beyond. Menchey's Spring is to the right.

Commanding the 17th Connecticut after Colonel Fowler's fall, Major Allen Brady reported: "We remained in...position [on the northern slope], exposed to the enemy's batteries and sharpshooters, until 7 p.m. when we were ordered to the extreme right, behind a stone wall on each side of a lane, below the battery opposite the cemetery entrance. Two companies were advanced to the grain field near the woods...." In their new position along Brickyard Lane, the New England regiment now faced the open meadows to the east, with von Gilsa's Brigade to their right and the 75th Ohio on their left.[2]

The regiment's move was not without incident. Still plying their trade in the fading light, the gray marksmen spied another target: "After I was ordered to the right with companies "C" and "D," while we were marching on the hillside, I was at the head in a Captain's place," wrote Lieutenant Milton Daniel, "and the orderly of Company "D" was at my side, a shot came—touched my coat—and took him in the side; he dropped dead. Soon the whole regiment was to the right behind a stone wall where brush had grown up by it. We had not been there long when we saw the rebs coming...."[3]

The construction of Wainwright Avenue would substantially alter the character of Brickyard Lane in this area as well. Just below the retaining wall, a bank of ground can be seen running alongside the modern road. This trace appears to indicate the original path of the lane as it crossed the face of the hill. The stone wall held by the 17th Connecticut ran along the western side of Brickyard Lane and was probably used in the construction of the modern retaining wall. Remain in this area for the following section of text.[4]

To the right of the 17th Connecticut, von Gilsa's line was still unsettled. Returning from positions in the fields to the east, the 41st New York formed on the right of the brigade line, with the 33rd Massachusetts taking position between the right of the New Yorkers and Whittier's Battery above. Returning to Brickyard Lane with the skirmishers of the 153rd Pennsylvania, Lt. Miller found the 41st New York in their

Turn-of-the-century Tipton photo looks south along Brickyard Lane beside the recently constructed Wainwright Avenue. The 17th Connecticut monument is visible on the right. (TC)

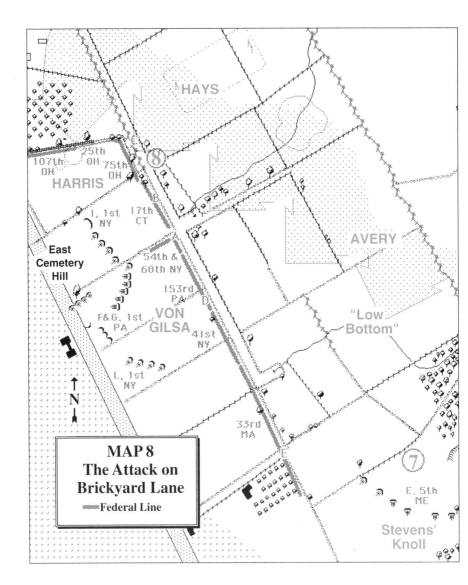

MAP 8
The Attack on
Brickyard Lane
▰▰▰ Federal Line

former position. As gunfire began to crackle along the wall, Miller spotted von Gilsa a short distance behind the line shouting, "Cease firing; they are our own men." "I reported that they were rebels, and asked for a position for my men," recalled Miller. "He pointed towards the wall towards the left from where we were standing; Lt. Barnes moved the men into position, when Gilsa again repeated the same command. I again told him it was the enemy and that I had been watching them all afternoon..." What Colonel von Gilsa thought of the upstart lieutenant was lost in the crash of a volley from the 153rd, who opened fire on the approaching Confederate lines.[5]

On von Gilsa's left, the officers of the 17th Connecticut were also having their share of problems directing fire in the half light. As Lt. Albert Peck described:

> *We had not been in our new position long when firing commenced on our picket line, and the pickets were driven in. Our boys commenced firing, when Major Brady ordered them to cease firing as we were firing on our own men; the firing ceased for a moment, when the boys saw the rebel line approaching and commenced firing again, and the batteries on the hill above us opened on them with grape and cannister, which passed over our heads.[6]*

Unfortunately, at least one of the Connecticut men also fell victim to the close support: "The battery in our rear was giving them a warm reception," Lt. Milton Daniel recalled, "the lead wadding from one shot killed one of our men, which demoralized us worse than the enemy in our front." Shortly after, Maj. Brady was struck in the shoulder by another piece of shell; reeling from the injury, Brady inadvertently injured another Connecticut man with his sword. But as the Confederate ranks came into view across the fields in their front, the Connecticut line settled down to business:

> *We had two men, one in Company "C," George Wood, Jr., the other William Curtis, of Newtown, who were particularly noticeable for coolness...While the Tigers were coming across the meadow, George and Bill were sitting down behind the stone wall, and you would have supposed they were shooting at a target. I saw George shoot from a dead rest, and heard him say, "He won't come any farther, will he, Bill?" Then Bill shot and said, "I got that fellow, George." And they kept it up that way perfectly oblivious to danger themselves.[7]*

Continue up Wainwright Avenue to the monument for the 25th and 75th Ohio located on your left (marked "C" on Maps 7 and 8). The flank markers visible to the left and on the hillside behind the monument approximate the positions held by these Ohio units in the following accounts (bear in mind that these slopes were largely clear of trees during the battle). The flank markers for the position of the 107th Ohio are on private land by the water tank at the top of the hill. Just visible in the half light and billowing smoke, the middle of Hays' line crossed the low ground to your right as it wheeled toward this position.[8]

Whatever its wisdom, the shifting of the Connecticut regiment had created a large gap in the Federal line between the 25th and 75th Ohio. Colonel Harris was ill-prepared for the new threat to his line:

Maj. Brady had no sooner reported to Gilsa with his regiment, when the assaulting columns of Early's division began to move...directly in the direction of my brigade. ...It was a complete surprise to us. We did not expect this assault as bravely and rapidly made. In fact, we did not expect any assault. We could not have been much more surprised if the moving column had raised up out of ground amid the waving timothy grass of the meadow. When the 17th Conn. was sent to Col. Gilsa, I was compelled to fill the vacancy left by it in my line, by thinning the line from the left, moving the regiments farther to the right except the left of the 107th Ohio. This left my line very thin and weak. All the men could get to the stonewall, used by us as a breastwork, and have all the elbow room he wanted...I rode along the line, and gave the men all the encouragement possible, told them of the importance of our position, and that we must hold it at all hazards.[9]

Hays' Louisianans pushed now toward the angle of Ames' position at the base of the hill. "When within 150 paces of us," Maj. Brady of the 17th Connecticut wrote, "we poured a

49

destructive fire upon them, which thinned their ranks and checked their advance. We fired several volleys by battalion, after which they charged upon us." Louisiana Captain William Seymour remembered, "Skirting the base of the Hill is a stone wall, from behind which a heavy line of Yankee infantry greet us with a destructive volley, and many of our noble fellows go down before it, killed or wounded; but our little command is not delayed by this impediment more than a minute."[10]

On the northern slope, the right of Hays' Brigade charged through knee-high corn with a Rebel yell, crashing into the Ohio line with bayonets leveled. "The right of Hays' Louisiana brigade [struck] my brigade just between the 107th and 25th Ohio," recalled Col. Harris. "At that point, and soon along my whole line the fighting was obstinate and bloody. The bayonet, club-musket, and anything in fact that could be made available was used, both by the assailing and their assailers." As the attack wore on the right of the 107th Ohio, the regiment "fell back fighting step by step to the stone fence in front of Wiedrich's 1st New York Battery...." "For a time the opposing forces were much mixed up together," wrote another Ohio veteran, "and with the uncertainty of the light, in the dusk of evening it was difficult to distinguish friend from foe."[11]

The terse accounts for the 25th Ohio do not say as such, but it is likely that their line was swept aside by the Louisiana troops. Of the sixty men reforming on Cemetery Hill the previous day, the regiment had lost an additional fourteen men to Southern skirmishers. Hastily arranged in a single rank at the stone wall running down the steep slope, the Ohio men now faced a swell in the hillside limiting their vision—and field of fire—across the hill. When Hays' battle line finally charged into sight, the matter was settled quickly. "We passed such of the enemy who had not fled, and were still clinging to the wall, to the rear, as prisoners," Hays recalled. "Still advancing, we came upon an abatis of fallen timber, and the third line, disposed in rifle pits. This line we broke, and as before, found many of the enemy who had not fled hiding in the pits for protection. These I ordered to the rear as prisoners, and continued my progress to the crest of the hill."[12]

STOP 8(c) – The 25th and 75th Ohio monument. The line of the 75th followed the wall at left up the hill to the flank markers (visible to the left and behind the monument). The 25th Ohio occupied the wall beyond.

"All the men could get to the stone wall and have all the elbow room he wanted..." Looking north from the flank markers for the 25th and 75th Ohio. Hays' Tigers charged through a cornfield on this slope and broke through the Federal line near here.

Flanked by the collapse of the 25th Ohio, part of the 75th Ohio's line was overrun, but the rest of the Buckeye regiment gamely held their position at the angle of the wall. Writing only days later, Sergeant Oscar Ladley recalled:

> *They came on us about dark yelling like demons with fixed bayonets. We opened on them...but still they came their officers & colors in advance. We lay behind a stone wall and received them with our bayonets. I was standing behind the wall when they came over. A Rebel officer made at me with a revolver with his colors by his side. I had no pistol nothing but my sword. Just as I was getting ready to strike him one of our boys run him through the body so saved me.* [13]

The account of another Ohio soldier is overwrought, but telling:

STOP 8(c) – *"We lay behind a stone wall and received them with our bayonets..." The view to the northeast today from behind the 75th Ohio's position. (RK)*

There stood the major of the Tigers! Right on top of the wall! He carried their flag! A flash of steel! Lorenzo Dowler stabbed the major through with his bayonet. The rebel fell headlong over the rocks as a force of his men sprang to the top of the wall... A lull for a minute or two. The Tiger's flag! What a scramble as the flag was torn to pieces! Our boys pounced on the rag as if a piece of it would be the greatest badge of bravery they would ever get their hands on. Andrew Jackson got the biggest piece. He shoved it in his pocket. He kept it as long as he lived, and gave it to one of his sons. Within an instant another charge by the Tigers! The wall, as far as I could see, was ablaze! Our color bearer was killed. We lost our flag and never had another. [Pvt. Lorenzo Dowler, Co. D, was killed the following year in Florida. Jackson, also a private in Company D, would be wounded six weeks later at Fort Wagner in S.C.][14]

At the stone wall to the right of the Ohioans, members of the 17th Connecticut grappled with the gray figures illuminated by the muzzle flashes of their muskets. Lt. Daniel later described one scene:

Corporal George Scott, who was acting orderly, had it hand to hand with the enemy as they charged the fence. He shot a fellow and took a captain prisoner. He had caught a Tiger; we did not know what to do with him; it was dusk and we had not the men to spare to send him to the rear, and I never knew how he was disposed of; I have often wondered....

Recently returned to the Connecticut regiment after being captured himself at Chancellorsville, Captain Henry Burr, "grabbed a 'Johnnie' by the collar of his coat during the fight, drew him over the wall and made him prisoner." Connecticut Private Moses Wheeler was less fortunate. Wrestling with one of the Southerners, Wheeler was dragged across the wall and sent across the meadow as a prisoner.[15]

If you drove to the turnout by the Ohio markers, you may remain in your vehicle, or walk as much of the following route as you wish. The tour will return to this position.

Walk back up Wainwright Avenue to the 54th New York monument (point "A", Maps 7 & 8) where you can view von Gilsa's position. Contemporary accounts of the action along this section of line are scant, and those available are confusing at best. Although von Gilsa's regiments shifted position frequently during their three days here, it does appear that the monuments approximate the brigade's position on the evening of July 2. (For further discussion on the Federal position here, see Appendix).[16]

Further down the lane, von Gilsa's line was coming apart. At the wall near the 17th Connecticut, the first to fall in the 54th New York was Color Sergeant Henry Michel. The next two men to take the flag fell in rapid succession, and the demoralized regiment known as the "Black Rifles" began to collapse. Seen from the 153rd Pennsylvania's position, "The first rebel line passed over and up towards the batteries; the second line [possibly Avery's] and our line met," Lt. Miller recalled.

> *The fight was on in all its fierceness, muskets being handled as clubs; rocks torn from the wall in front and thrown, fist and bayonets used, so close was the fighting. I remember distinctly of seeing a Rebel color bearer, with his musket in one hand and flag in the other, with outspread arms jump upon the little wall, shouting, 'Surrender, you damned Yankees.' In an instant a Company A or F man, I could not tell which, as the smoke was commencing to get heavy,—ran his bayonet through the man's chest and firing at the same time. I can still see in my mind's eye how the shot tore into shreds the back of his blouse....[17]*

"About this time, quite a number of the enemy forced me and some of my Company with others of the N.Y. regiment on my right [the 41st New York], up into our batteries," wrote Miller afterward. "Here the mix-up of artillery-

1880's Tipton photo from the early observation tower looks east over the low ground crossed by Hays' men. The modern stadium is located beyond the fence at left center. The lunette marking Cooper's and Ricketts' left flank is in the foreground.

men, cavalry [probably drivers for the batteries], infantry and rebels was something long to be remembered."[18]

Contributing to the shaky condition of von Gilsa's line was the rise of ground some 100 paces east of the right center of his line. As on the hillside to the north, Federals along Brickyard Lane in this area could see little of the enemy line as it headed toward their position. For those who had survived the debacle of July 1 and the sunset attack at Chancellorsville just two months before, the uproar on the hillside behind them combined with the sounds of the approaching Confederate line may well have been enough. Although some of the Union line held on long enough to send volleys into the gray ranks, most of von Gilsa's Brigade, "commenced running in the greatest confusion to the rear," claimed Captain R. Bruce Ricketts, "and so panic stricken that several ran into the canister fire of my guns and were knocked over."[19]

From Charles Wainwright's perspective on the crest, his infantry supports had vanished: "I pitied General Ames most heartily. His men would not stand at all, save one. I believe not a single regiment of the Eleventh Corps exposed to the attack stood fire, but ran away almost to a man." But out of Wainwright's sight at the nose of the hill, Harris' last two regiments, the 17th Connecticut and 75th Ohio, still vied with the center of Hays' line. "Only about half a dozen of the enemy broke through," recalled young Lt. Daniel, "but the dead in front were in heaps."[20]

Continue walking back up Wainwright Avenue along von Gilsa's position. Note the fields beyond the wall to the east. Although the rolling ground sheltered the advancing Confederate line to some degree, the uneven terrain also made it difficult to maintain order on the dark hillside. Stop in the area of the 153rd Pennsylvania monument for the next section (marked "D" on Maps 7 and 8).

BREAKTHROUGH

"THE HOUR WAS ONE OF HORROR..."

Despite the great gap in von Gilsa's line, the long advance was taking its toll on the Confederate regiments. Closing on the hill in the fading light, Avery's Brigade crossed into the area of uneven ground surrounding the eastern base of Cemetery Hill. "In swinging around, three stone walls had to be surmounted. The ground was rocky and uneven," recalled Godwin, "and these obstacles prevented the rapidity of movement and unity of action which might have insured success."[1]

From the saddle above, Whittier's six Napoleons on McKnight's Hill raked the North Carolina ranks with canister—containers holding about twenty-five lead balls that spread like lethal buck shot. "At 8:30 we had an oblique fire on them," Lt. Whittier wrote, "and when they were under the steep acclivity of Cemetery Hill...the Fifth Maine had an enfilading fire on their whole left and centre." By Southern accounts however, the damage was less than Whittier supposed. The failing light and broken terrain, the very factors that created such havoc in the advance, now proved a blessing. "We were now within canister range," General Hays later wrote, "but owing to the darkness of the evening, now verging into night, and the deep obscurity afforded by the smoke of the firing, our exact locality could not be discovered by the enemy's gunners, and thus we escaped what in the full light of day would have been nothing more else than horrible slaughter." "The enemy's batteries kept up a terrific fire, but most of the shells and grape passed over our heads," wrote Pvt. Thomas Causby of the 6th North Carolina.

> *Our brigade charged in good order until we were within a short distance of the stone fence, which did not extend all the way across the face of the hill. Here the brigade spread out across the face of the hill, part of the men making for the end of the fence, as I recollect. About seventy-five of our brigade, led by Colonel Tate and Captain Neill Ray, charged directly on the stone fence, which we crossed and then bayoneted the*

Yankee gunners and drove them back after a hard fight. About twenty men attached to the Louisiana brigade crossed the fence at the same time we did.[2]

Marked by the line of brush about seventy-five yards away are the traces of a stone wall running partially across the field parallel to the road. (In 1863, this wall connected with a wooden fenceline that continued northward. See Map 8). This may well be the stone wall skirted by the 6th North Carolina in Causby's account.

To the left of the 6th North Carolina, the 21st North Carolina had lost four color bearers and all but one of its field officers. Major James Beall wrote:

The ground we had to pass over was ascending, but the troops advanced in double quick time, and with a cheer went over the rifle pits in advance of the enemy's main line of works, killing and capturing a few of them—the greater part taking refuge behind the main line of breastworks. ...The ground was strewn with dead and wounded. Man after man went down, among them Major Alexander Miller, who picked up the flag after the first color-bearer fell. He soon shared the fate of the former. It was soon taken up by J. W. Bennett, Company F, who was also, in quick succession, shot down. The colors were then taken by the writer....[3]

Proceed up Wainwright Avenue toward Stevens' Knoll. The walls above Menchey's Spring would be occupied by the 41st New York and the 33rd Massachusetts only minutes before the attack (the placement of the regimental monuments is approximate). Near the intersection with Slocum Avenue, stop by the 33rd Massachusetts monument and view the low ground beyond the fenceline for the following accounts (marked "E" on Maps 7 and 8).

"The ground we had to pass over was ascending..." 1863 photo looking north from the slope of Stevens' Knoll. Avery's men charged over this ground toward Brickyard Lane located behind the trees at left. (TC)

The terrain east of Cemetery Hill today.

"The Tigers were coming across the meadow..." Terrain west of the wall occupied by von Gilsa's 41st New York. The line of brush and small trees in the field beyond cover the partial wall mentioned in the text.

On the far left, Colonel Godwin and the 57th North Carolina reached, "a low bottom," in the ravine just below McKnight's Hill (marked on Maps 7 and 8). Lagging behind the rest of the line, the left of the regiment was forced to "swing round almost half a turn before it struck the face of the ridge." wrote Colonel H. C. Jones. "In the meantime the Sixth and Twenty-first Regiments and the right battalion of the Fifty-Seventh had reached the foot of the ridge and were driving the enemy from his entrenchments up the hill...."[4]

Overlooking the North Carolinians from McKnight's Hill, Lt. Whittier watched the Southerners attempting to reform below:

> *It was now so dark that the enemy's line could be made out only by the fire of their rifles. The extreme left, bent back, nearly faced us, but their left and centre were still facing the slopes of Cemetery Hill, and a desperate effort was made by their officers...to rally a sufficient number of their men to enable them to secure a foothold among the batteries.*

As the Confederate line passed to the left of the 5th Maine, Whittier realigned his guns to face north—no doubt a tricky maneuver on the dark, crowded hilltop:

> *The trails of the guns of the left half of the battery were swung sharp and hard to the right, the right half battery was limbered to the rear, and in the darkness hurried into position on the left of the guns remaining in the works, and in a moment the whole battery was pouring a most destructive, demoralizing, enfilading fire of double canister into a confused mass of the enemy struggling in the uncertain shadows of the crest of Cemetery Hill.*

Responding to the new threat to their line, the North Carolinians sent a volley up the smoke-filled slope, killing four of the six-horse team of Whittier's left piece.[5]

Just below the Maine battery, the 41st New York and the 33rd Massachusetts still held the section of stone wall on von Gilsa's right flank. Commanding the 33rd Massa-

"We drove the enemy from his last stone wall..." Part of Von Gilsa's position photographed shortly after the battle. The stone wall behind the small tree at center borders Brickyard Lane. The walls bordering Menchey's Spring are visible on the right.

chusetts, Colonel Adin Underwood could make out the North Carolinians climbing the steep ravine in front of the Bay State regiment:

> *The enemy came on gallantly unchecked by our artillery fire, and my regiment opened a severe musketry fire on them, which caused great gaps in their line and made it stagger back a little. It soon rallied and bravely came within a few feet of our wall, though my men clung unflinchingly to it and steadily poured in their fire. I ordered them to fix bayonets to be ready for the enemy but at this time Stevens' Maine battery...to my right, opened on them at point blank range, and with*

this fire and the continued fire of my regiment, the enemy's line said to be Hoke's brigade of North Carolinians, which was almost onto us, their colors nearly within reach, was broken....[6]

To the left of the Massachusetts regiment, the rout along Brickyard Lane had reached the left wing of the 41st New York. "The enemy came so far as to break through the line, which was kept by either the Sixty-eighth Regiment New York Volunteers or the Fifty-fourth Regiment, and move[d] on toward the batteries," wrote Lieutenant Colonel von Einsiedel. "In this critical moment, Capt. Alfred Theinhardt...took two companies of the Forty-first New York which he placed with some men of other regiments...behind a stone wall." As Theinhardt's men reformed along the stone wall perpendicular to the road, the New York line took "the form of a triangle," according to one veteran. For better or worse, the New Yorkers were now able to rake the Tarheels' flank as they climbed the slope.[7]

Modern appearance of von Gilsa's position along Wainwright Avenue. The 41st New York marker is at center of view.

"The enemy's batteries now enfiladed us," wrote Colonel A. C. Godwin of the 57th North Carolina, "and a destructive fire was poured into our ranks from a line of infantry formed in the rear of a stone wall running at a right angle with our line of battle." Probably leading companies from the right of the regiment, Godwin somehow managed to skirt the harrowing fire from the hillside. "The men now charged up the hill with heroic determination, and drove the enemy from his last stone wall," Godwin reported. "In this charge, the command had become much separated, and in the darkness it was now found impossible to concentrate more than 40 or 50 men at any point for further advance." Attempting to rally his men in the murk, Godwin came face to face with a large Federal who "attempted to brain him," with his musket. The six-foot-tall Godwin deflected the Northerner's rifle with his left arm, "nearly decapitated his adversary with a blow from his sword," and continued across the hillside.[8]

Major James Beall of the 21st North Carolina recalled the moment like a glimpse from some nightmare:

> *The hour was one of horror. Amid the incessant roar of the cannon, the din of musketry, and the glare of bursting shells making the darkness intermittent— adding awfulness to the scene—the hoarse shouts of friend and foe, piteous cries of the wounded and dying, one could well imagine...that "war is hell."*[9]

STOP 1 (Map 2; Map 9 for 1863 appearance) ━━━━━
Return to your vehicle now. (If you left your vehicle on Stevens' Knoll, return and drive down the hill, retracing your path along Wainwright Avenue past the turnout by the Ohio monument). Follow Wainwright Avenue to the stop sign at Lefever Street and turn left. At the next stop sign, turn left back onto Baltimore Street. Bear left at the next light, and return to the parking area at the top of East Cemetery Hill. Proceed on foot to the area behind Wiedrich's Battery for the next section (marked "A" on Map 2). Keep in mind that by the time the fighting reached this point on July 2, the hilltop was shrouded in darkness and thick smoke.

The Struggle for the Crest

"With Bayonet, Clubbed-Musket and Rocks..."

While the Connecticut and Ohio regiments struggled with the Southerners at the bottom of the hill, Hays' right wing pushed on toward Wiedrich's battery. There the Tigers again clashed with Federal infantry. Lieutenant Jackson of the 8th Louisiana recalled:

With bayonets & clubbed guns we drove them back, by this time it was dark & we couldn't tell whether we were shooting our own men or theirs. Capt. Duchamp the color bearer was wounded & Leon Gusman carried the colors up to the battery and planted them on the breastworks, he was then wounded or taken & our colors lost—Willis had a hand to hand fight with a Yank and took his colors away from him.

Across the hillside from Jackson, Captain Peter Young of the 107th Ohio was part of the melee:

An order now came to fall back upon the battery and hold that at all hazards. (At this time our brave Color bearer, Sergt. Geibel who stood flaunting them in the faces of the rebels, was shot and it was fortunate that I could save the colors from rebel grasp;) and having scaled the stone-fence on our right, found the rebels up to and among our guns, yelling like demons at the supposed capture...I ran forward, revolver in hand, shot down the color bearer (8" La. Tiger Regt. as it proved by the inscription on the vile rag) and sprang for the colors, at the same time a rebel, seeing his comrade fall, sprang forward and caught them but fell to the ground, where I wrested them from him. These in one hand and revolver in the other, I was in the act of turning towards our men, when a rebel bullet pierced my left lung and arm; the turning saved me from falling and rebel bayonets undoubtedly, for I kept on my feet till I reached our men when all strength left me and my Sergt. Maj. Henry Brinker caught me in his arms as I was falling.

Unknown to Young, a Louisiana officer pursued him back to his line, sword at the ready, until he was brought down with a saber blow from an Ohio lieutenant.[1]

Follow Wiedrich's position to the right, and cross the stone wall to the next line of guns. Occupied by Cooper's Battery for most of July 2, these lunettes mark the positions taken by Captain R. B. Ricketts' guns just before the Confederate advance.

Across the wall from Wiedrich's now silent battery, Ricketts' guns still sprayed rounds of canister across the slope in their front. Running out of canister, the Pennsylvanians resorted to "rotten shot"—rounds of case shot fired without fuses, allowing the rounds to burst prematurely at the muzzle of the gun. To their left, despite determined resistance from Wiedrich's men and the rallied infantry, the Louisianans gained the wall between the two Pennsylvania batteries. There they delivered a galling fire into Ricketts' gunners. "Our left piece, which was close to the stone-wall, was spiked by the enemy," one artillerist remembered, "but only after they had killed, wounded or taken prisoners every man belonging to it." Severely wounded in the melee, Lt. William Thurston, survived only by laying under the gun as the fight swirled over him. "Even when the left half of the battery was engaged in a hand to hand fight with the rebels who had leaped the stone wall," recalled Capt. Ricketts, "the fire was kept up by the right half."[2]

On the east face of the hill, isolated groups of Louisiana and North Carolina troops made the long climb up the slope. Unsupported and out of communication with the rest of Hays' line, "...75 North Carolinians of the Sixth Regiment and 12 Louisianians of Hays' brigade scaled the walls and planted the colors of the Sixth North Carolina and Ninth Louisiana on the guns. It was now fully dark," Major Samuel Tate remembered. "The enemy stood with a tenacity never before displayed by them, but with bayonet, clubbed musket, sword, and pistol, and rocks from the wall, we cleared the heights and silenced the guns."³

Continue walking along Ricketts' position to the area behind the center two guns. Occupied by the limbers of Lieutenant Frank Brockway's section, this area is described in the following account.

The Southerners spilled into the Pennsylvania battery from two sides. "The scene was now one of the wildest confusion," wrote Lieutenant Brockway of Battery F. "Friends and foes were indiscriminately mixed, and our brave men, though outnumbered and without arms, by means of handspikes, rammers and stones...made a sturdy resistance." At Ricketts' third piece, Brockway joined the fight for another prize:

> *A rebel first Lieutenant attempted to seize our battery guidon...but while in the act of grasping it, the bearer James H. Riggin, rode up and with his revolver shot the officer through the body. Seizing the colors he wheeled his horse, but at the same moment was shot himself, and died soon after. A Serg't of the "Tigers" got clear back to the limbers, and there caught Riggin's horse, and picked up the fallen colors. While leading back the horse he was encountered by Serg't. Stratford, who, unable to recognize him [in] the dark, demanded to know "where he was going with that horse." The rebel brought his musket to his shoulder and demanded Stratford's surrender. At this moment I walked up, and a glance showed me the true state of affairs. Having no side arms by me, I picked up a stone, and in a most unmilitary manner, broke the fellow's head. He tumbled to the ground, but Stratford, not knowing the cause, seized his musket and shot him in the abdomen. Fearing he had missed him in the darkness, he clubbed the musket, and broke the fellow's arm whereupon he asked for "quarter"...I don't think he lived long.⁴*

Although badly disorganized by the long assault and limited visibility, the remnants of Hays' and Avery's brigades had gained a foothold on East Cemetery Hill. "Arriving at the summit, by a simultaneous rush from my whole line, I captured several pieces of artillery, four stand of colors, and a number of prisoners," General Hays reported. "At that time every piece of artillery that had been firing on us was silenced. A quiet of several minutes now ensued." Hays' aide, Captain William Seymour, later wrote, "Gen. Hays immediately reformed his line, and anxiously waited to hear Rodes' guns co-operating with us on the right; but, unfortunately, no such assistance came to us."[5]

In the fields to the west of Cemetery Hill, the anticipated attack by Major General Robert Rodes' Division had barely begun. During the day, three of Rodes' brigades under Ramseur, Iverson and Doles were positioned in the streets of Gettysburg. That afternoon, Rodes received orders to "co-operate with the attacking force as soon as any opportunity of doing so with good effect was offered." At that point, Rodes still had time to march his large division clear of Gettysburg, turn south again and wheel through the fields southwest of the town to face Cemetery Hill. With the strange lethargy

Panoramic view of the area north and northeast of East Cemetery Hill after the battle. The German Reformed Church is at center; the Culp farm is visible

that plagued many of the Southern attacks that day, Rodes waited until Early had started his advance before moving his division from the town.[6]

By the time Rodes' three brigades pushed in the Yankee skirmish line at the foot of Cemetery Hill, the moon had risen and Early's attack had long since peaked. Within two hundred yards of the hill, Rodes' brigade commanders could make out a formidable—and intact—Federal position on Cemetery Hill. "These facts, together with Early's withdrawal, of which I had been officially informed, and the increased darkness," Rodes later wrote, "convinced me that it would be a useless sacrifice of life to go on, and a recall was ordered."[7]

In the meantime, Early's reserve brigade under Brigadier General John B. Gordon moved to a support position near Winebrenner's Run. Realizing that no reinforcements would be coming from the right, Early halted the six Georgia regiments to avoid further "useless sacrifice of life." The small bands of Louisiana and North Carolina men would have to defend their foothold on East Cemetery Hill alone—the only reinforcements approaching the hilltop wore Union blue.[8]

on the far right. The ridge that hid Hays' and Avery's brigades is discernible at the right middle of view. (TC)

69

THE REPULSE

"HOW ANXIOUSLY WE LOOKED FOR REINFORCEMENTS..."

Strangely, Colonel Harris of the Ohio brigade was not the only one surprised by Early's assault on East Cemetery Hill. While conferring with General Howard, Schurz remembered: "We suddenly heard a rapid musketry fire on the eminence immediately east of the cemetery, where Captain Wiedrich's battery stood." Sending word of the attack to headquarters, Howard then ordered Schurz to East Cemetery Hill with reinforcements. Followed by Kryzanowski's 58th and 119th New York, and the remnants of Coster's Brigade, Schurz and his staff charged across the hill:

> Soon we found ourselves surrounded by a rushing crowd of stragglers from the already broken lines. We did our best, sword in hand, to drive them back as we went. Arriving at the batteries, we found an indescribable scene of melee. Some rebel infantry had scaled the breastworks, and were taking possession of the guns. But the cannoneers defended themselves desperately. With rammers and fence rails, hand spikes and stones, they knocked down the intruders.... Our infantry made a vigorous rush upon the invaders, and after a short but spirited hand-to-hand scuffle tumbled them down the embankment.[1]

Meanwhile, some 600 yards to the southwest, the last wave of Longstreet's four-hour-old assault had broken against Hancock's Second Corps line on Cemetery Ridge. As the firing died down in his front, Hancock became concerned by the commotion on the heights to his rear. Whether driven by Howard's request or a soldier's intuition, Hancock directed three regiments of his reserve brigade under Colonel Samuel S. Carroll to proceed toward Cemetery Hill. Carroll hastily formed his brigade into column, with the 14th Indiana followed by the 7th West Virginia and 4th Ohio. Charles Myerhoff of the 14th Indiana recalled, "We were moved from

70

Ziegler's Grove over the Taneytown Pike, up the hill into the cemetery. While passing through the cemetery it became quite dusk, and when nearing the Baltimore Pike the flying missiles were making a fearful spattering on the tombstones." Clearing Osborn's artillery posted in the cemetery, Carroll's men reached the Baltimore Pike south of the gatehouse and formed their line.[2]

Looking toward the gatehouse of Evergreen Cemetery, the monument to Carroll's 4th Ohio is at the wall to your left (the guns beyond the wall mark the position of Reynolds' 1st New York, Battery L). Monuments to Carroll's 14th Indiana and 7th West Virginia are near the wall to your right. In the following accounts, the center of Carroll's charge crossed onto East Cemetery Hill and headed toward your position (See Map 9).

The 14th Indiana's line pushed into the darkness on East Cemetery Hill, "covering the whole of Reynolds' battery and the right of Ricketts' guns." "Owing to the artillery fire from our own guns, it was impossible to advance by a longer front than that of a regiment," Carroll reported, "and it being perfectly dark, and with no guide, I had to find the enemy's line entirely by their fire." Receiving flank fire from Hays' men at the wall between the batteries, Carroll quickly sent the 7th West Virginia to the left of the Indiana regiment, while the 4th Ohio swung out to the right.[3]

Arriving independently, and within minutes of each other, regiments from two Federal corps now advanced across the breadth of East Cemetery Hill. General Hays later wrote:

Their heavy masses of infantry were heard and perfectly discerned through the increasing darkness, advancing in the direction of my position. Approaching within 100 yards, a line was discovered before us, from the whole length of which a simultaneous fire was delivered. I reserved my fire, from the uncertainty of this being a force of the enemy or a force of our men, as I had been cautioned to expect friends both in front, to the right, and to

71

the left...but after the delivery of a second and third vol-
ley, the flashing of the musketry disclosed the still ad-
vancing line to be one of the enemy.

"I then gave the order to fire; the enemy was checked for a time," Hays wrote, "but discovering another line moving up in the rear of this one, and still another force in the rear of that, and being beyond the reach of support, I gave the order to retire to the stone wall at the foot of the hill, which was quietly and orderly effected."[4]

By 8:45 p.m., a full moon was rising from behind Culp's Hill, but little light penetrated the thick clouds of smoke on the hillside. In front of Ricketts' guns, the isolated pockets of North Carolinians began to withdraw down the slope. In his report for the 6th North Carolina, Major Tate recalled: "Finding the enemy were moving up in a line, I ordered the small band of heroes to fall back from the crest to a stone wall on the side of the hill, where we awaited their coming." Just across the slope, Captain Neill Ray awaited the Federal advance:

> *It was then after daylight had gone down, the smoke was very dense, and although the moon was rising, we could not see what the enemy was doing, but we could hear him attempting to rally his men, and more than once he rallied close up to us. But our men formed behind a rock wall, and as he approached we fired a volley into him, which drove him back. This occurred at least twice. No one who has never been in a similar position can understand how anxiously we looked for reinforcements. None came, however....*[5]

Nearby, the 21st North Carolina had lost all of its field officers but one, and only a small band under Major Beall clung to the hillside near the breastworks:

> *We fell back to the works, which we had just passed over a few paces and continued such a terrific fire upon the enemy, that their rifle fire was completely silenced....About this time Corporal Eli Wiley, Company M, asked permission to take the flag...It was given to him and after the writer had gone a few paces along the line, orders were given to retire at once, which was accomplished under a severe fusillade. We had re-*

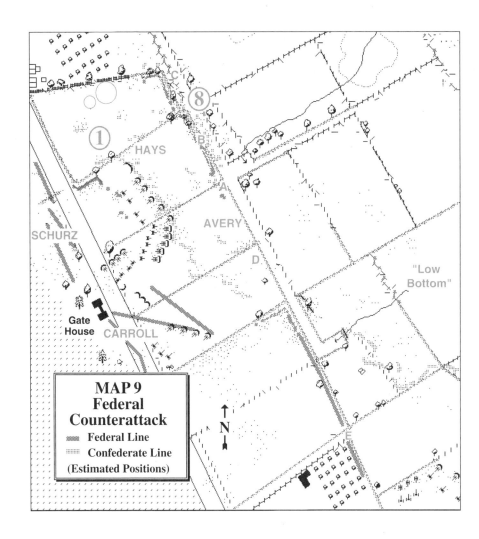

MAP 9
Federal
Counterattack
▨ Federal Line
░ Confederate Line
(Estimated Positions)

*treated about twenty-five yards when I saw the flag for
the last time. Corporal Wiley was killed and left, together with the flag, in the lines of the enemy. In the
darkness and confusion the flag was not missed until
we had rallied under cover about the distance of two
hundred yards.[6]*

Charging down the hill, the 14th Indiana captured about
twenty members of the North Carolina regiment, as well as the
Tarheels' missing banner. But their advance was costly. In its
brief foray across East Cemetery Hill, the Indiana regiment had
taken thirty-one casualties, including six men killed.[7]

"Final Charge of the Union Forces On Cemetery Hill" – A 1865 lithograph.

The area in the lithograph today.

Modern view looks toward the Evergreen Cemetery gatehouse from Wiedrich's battery. Carroll's 7th West Virginia (monument at center) and Eleventh Corps regiments drove Hays' men from their foothold here.

Reclaiming their guns, Ricketts' and Wiedrich's gunners sent loads of canister into the murk beyond Brickyard Lane. "Had it not been for the darkness," Hays' adjutant William Seymour later wrote," the enemy would have, no doubt, cut us up terribly with his re-captured artillery as we fell back down the hill." To those in the ranks, the explanation was plain: "It was soon so dark that we couldent see what we was a doing," a North Carolina sergeant penned in his diary. "And the enemy got to geather again and we had no reinforcement and we had to fall back to our old position."[8]

Returning to Winebrenner's Run, Hays found Gordon's Brigade in his former position, and reformed his Louisianans on High Street near the German Reformed Church. In his hospital nearby, Private Silliman watched their return. "The clash was tremendous, but short, and Jackson's picked men [Early's division was formerly part of Major General T. J. "Stonewall" Jackson's Corps] retreated back panic stricken and with their ranks terribly thinned. Then [it] was that we were gladdened by the cheers of our men. The fight raged till nearly nine o'clock."

Avery's shaken brigade, now led by Colonel Godwin, withdrew back across the meadow and reformed along the railroad where their prospects had seemed so promising just the previous evening.[9]

Across the meadows from Silliman's hospital, the full moon shone brightly over the Culp's Hill and, one Union veteran recalled that, "in its light the field took on a weird and ghastly aspect." Carroll's 14th Indiana and 4th Ohio reformed on Brickyard Lane at the wall formerly held by von Gilsa's regiments. Stopping their drive on the hillside below Wiedrich's guns, the 7th West Virginia reformed facing north along the wall above the Indiana regiment. Relieved by Carroll's men, the 75th Ohio and 17th Connecticut reformed and filed into position on the right flank of the rest of the Ohio Brigade, now facing the town at the wall north of Wiedrich's Battery. "We gathered up the dead and cared for the wounded of both friend and foe," Colonel Harris reported. "This closed the fight so far as our brigade was concerned."[10]

The flat stone marking the spot where the 7th West Virginia ended its charge can be seen on the hillside in front of Wiedrich's guns. Small markers along Wainwright Avenue indicating the final positions for Carroll's regiments are situated along von Gilsa's line. If you wish, you may return to your vehicle to complete the text.

EPILOGUE

The major action at Gettysburg shifted on July 3 to another series of futile attacks on the Federal right at Culp's Hill, and Lee's climactic assault on the center of Meade's line. Those who had struggled for East Cemetery Hill spent another day at the mercy of sharpshooters' bullets and shelling from enemy batteries, but for most, the fighting at Gettysburg had ended. On July 4, the Ohio Brigade would be the first to re-enter Gettysburg to find that Lee had withdrawn Ewell's Corps from the town—the start of their long trek back to Virginia.

Only hours after the gunfire stopped, recriminations began over the action on East Cemetery Hill. In his journal of the battle, Hays' adjutant noted, "The charge was a daring and desperate one, and, although unsuccessful on account of the failure of our supports to come up, we gained great credit for it.... This want of concert of action on the part of our Generals was the chief cause of the loss of the great battle of Gettysburg," Captain Seymour wrote, "the Army was fought by Divisions instead of Corps, which was a great and unfortunate mistake."[1]

Accused of retreating "to a man," blame fell heavily on the Eleventh Corps for the near disaster on Cemetery Hill. After the debacle at Chancellorsville the previous month, few were interested in taking further chances on the "Unlucky Eleventh." Within three months of Gettysburg, the Army of the Potomac would divest itself of Howard's Corps, transferring one division to South Carolina and the balance to the Army of the Cumberland in the western theater.

As time went by, the eminence at the center of the Union line continued to be a source of controversy. A seemingly endless series of arguments about the action would be tossed around campfires, at reunions, and in letters and newspaper articles for years after the war.[2]

The remaining certainty is the loss suffered by both armies in the attack on East Cemetery Hill. Avery's North Carolinians were particularly hard hit, losing fully one third of their number—412 men—over half from the 6th North Carolina alone. Virtually all of these North Carolinians' losses occurred during the attack on July 2. Hays' five Louisiana regiments lost 334 men at Gettysburg, just over a quarter of those engaged.[3]

Due to the heavy casualties received on the first day, the losses incurred by Howard's men in the defense of East Cemetery Hill are difficult to determine. Unengaged in the first day's fighting, von Gilsa's 41st New York is at least indicative of the destruction. Arriving on the field with 218 men, the New Yorkers lost a third of their number on Cemetery Hill alone. At the other side of the hill, the 25th Ohio lost 160 of its original 220 members on July 1. By July 4, all of its officers were dead or wounded, and the thirty-six remaining members were led by Lt. John Milliman, who himself was wounded the first day. In all, Ames' two brigades lost over half—1,305 of the 2,473 men engaged—in the course of the battle.[4]

Before you leave the area, take a moment to read the following excerpt from a guidebook published ten years after the battle. Despite the many changes in the years since, the description of this area is as fitting now as it was in 1873:

What is there in this beautiful locality to indicate that it is the theatre where was once enacted such a fearful drama? What in this old stone wall to attract the attention of the passerby? Yet here, where the grass grows so freshly,...brothers, who should have extended the friendly grasp, frenzied by the maddening influences of political strife, with the mania of savage beasts, writhed and strove in mortal combat...this episode will perhaps convey a faint idea of the horror of a three days contest which extended over a field like this.

—Colonel John B. Bachelder[5]

(RK)

APPENDIX

THE BRICKYARD LANE POSITION

At first glance, the orderly arrangement of the monuments along Wainwright Avenue seems straightforward enough (see Map 7). However, when this tidy picture is combined with contemporary accounts, the position of the Northern regiments during the attack on July 2 is more elusive. In the analysis that follows, a number of sources have been combined to provide a "best guess" about the Federal position at Brickyard Lane. Obviously, no definitive answers are possible here. It is hoped new information will come to light that will allow us to understand the struggle at the foot of East Cemetery Hill more clearly.

Source Information

The Monuments

The most imposing evidence available on the Federal position, the regimental monuments and flank markers, should provide a basis for examining the site. But how accurately do these century-old memorials indicate the positions of individual units? A large measure of historical accuracy was ensured in the 1880s when guidelines for the placement and inscription of regimental memorials were instituted by the original Gettysburg Battlefield Memorial Association. Under this system, monuments were to be approved and placed in the position occupied by the regiment when it went into action. Secondary or advanced positions held by a unit were to be indicated by another smaller marker.

Despite the relative success of this system in marking the field, some of its drawbacks become apparent in examining the positions on Wainwright Avenue: (1) the monuments do not reflect subsequent (or previous) shifts within a brigade line; (2) a monument need not indicate the same time period as another marker only yards away; (3) clearly, site adjustments were made to allow for the construction of modern avenues and the requirements of the memorials themselves; and, (4) obviously all the participants would not agree on where they were in the course of a battle.

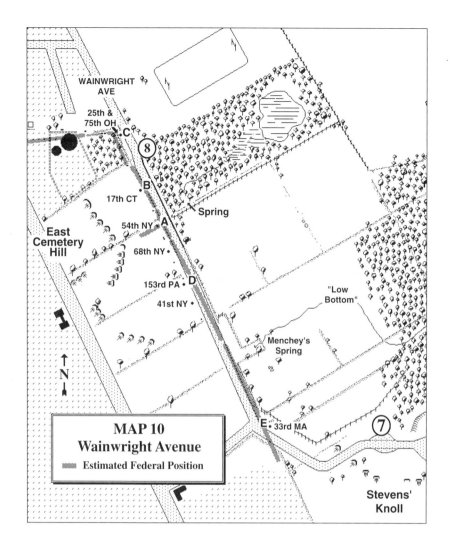

WAINWRIGHT AVE

25th & 75th OH

C

8

B

17th CT

Spring

54th NY **A**

68th NY

East Cemetery Hill

153rd PA **D**

41st NY

"Low Bottom"

Menchey's Spring

N

E 33rd MA

7

**MAP 10
Wainwright Avenue**

▨ Estimated Federal Position

Stevens' Knoll

The Bachelder Maps

One of the earliest comprehensive sources of information on the battlefield, the maps produced by Colonel John Bachelder in 1876 delineated troop positions using information provided by the veterans themselves. As Superintendent of Tablets and Legends for GBMA, Bachelder would also oversee the monumentation of the field during the 1880s. Consequently, while the placement of markers is fairly consistent with these maps, some of the same liabilities are present as well. For the purposes of this overview, the regimental positions as drawn by Bachelder are interpreted literally. (Unless noted, all regimental positions are drawn from the map labeled "Second Day's Battle").

Written Accounts
Not surprisingly, there are several discrepancies between the arrangement of monuments on East Cemetery Hill and those described in primary sources. This information is drawn largely from statements made in official reports filed shortly after the battle, and in letters and speeches written subsequently by the combatants. Unfortunately, relatively few of the extant accounts describe the actions along Brickyard Lane, and fewer still clearly detail the positions of individual units.

Regiment Size
In order to get some idea of space required for each unit on the hillside, regimental strengths for the evening of July 2 were estimated. When no contemporary quotes of regimental strength were available for July 2 (almost every case), an estimate was derived by subtracting two-thirds of those reported killed and wounded, and almost all those captured, from previous roster figures to account for the heavy losses on the first day. Assuming each regiment was arranged in a conventional double-ranked line, this number was then divided in half to estimate the number of men in one rank. Multiplying this figure by 2.5 feet provides a rough estimate of the space required for that regiment. In the summaries that follow, the unit designation is followed by the regiment's estimated strength as well as the measured distance between the flank markers. (All estimates are based on figures from Busey and Martin's *Regimental Strengths and Losses at Gettysburg*).

Regimental Positions

Harris' Brigade (2nd Brig., 1st Div., 11th Corps)
107th Ohio [*~292 members / 97 ft.*] The position of the regiment is indicated by two flank markers on the north side of East Cemetery Hill (oddly, there is no other monument to the regiment on the hill). The position as marked seems very small, even for the 171 members reported by Captain Young for the night of July 1 (no doubt some of those missing turned up later). Although this position is

East Cemetery Hill from Culp's Hill Tower. (TC)

consistent with the "board fence" mentioned in the regiment's accounts, the Bachelder map places the left of the regiment closer to the Baltimore Pike; this seems to make more sense for the size of this regiment.

25th Ohio [*~60 members / 136 ft.*] Identified by flank markers on the right of the 107th Ohio, the position marked here coincides with Colonel Harris' report and apparently indicates where the line of the 25th Ohio stretched down the slope after the shift of the 17th Connecticut. The position as marked is too large for a conventional defense, but would easily hold the single rank of Ohioans described by Harris.

75th Ohio [*~113 members / 125 ft.*] Located adjacent to the 25th Ohio, the position marked for the 75th Ohio is at the northeast angle of Ames' position (the 25th and 75th Ohio share the large memorial here). The Bachelder map places the entire regiment along Brickyard Lane in this area, but not in the L-shaped arrangement indicated by the markers. However, the space available between the flank markers is appropriate for a regiment of this size.

17th Connecticut [*~223 members / 277 ft.—no flank markers*] This monument stands on Wainwright Avenue between the right of the 75th Ohio and von Gilsa's left flank. The location coincides with regimental accounts and the space available here on von Gilsa's flank is more than large enough for this regiment. However, Major Brady's report mentions forming along "a wall on each side of a lane." It would seem Brady refers to the old farm lane that ran perpendicular to the road (see text), but Bachelder places the regiment diagonally across Brickyard Lane with their center about where the marker is. As mentioned in the text, the construction of Wainwright Avenue dramatically altered the landscape in this area (see note #4, Brickyard Lane chapter).

Von Gilsa's Brigade (1st Brig., 1st Div., 11th Corps)
54th New York [*~105 members / 134 ft.*] Located on the right of the 17th Connecticut, the monument stands on a hillock on the slope above Wainwright Avenue. The position marked by the flank stones would accommodate two ranks of this regiment, but other information does not confirm the

The fresh water spring located in front of the 54th New York monument. The head of the spring is now hidden beneath by the logs at right center.

orientation of the markers, at least not for the evening of July 2. The Bachelder map depicts the regiment's line as refused (at a right angle to the lane) and occupying the wall running uphill from their memorial. There seems to be no documentary evidence from the regiment itself, but one of the more prolific writers on the action, Lt. Edward Whittier of the 5th Maine Battery, confirmed Bachelder's placement in 1891 (although one might wonder if he drew his information from the map itself). In an 1886 letter to Bachelder, Lt. J. C. Miller of the 153rd Pennsylvania describes going to a spring "in front of the 54th and 68th [New York]," possibly the one located here on the east side of the lane (see 153rd PA).

68th New York [*~116 members / 109 ft.*] Located adjacent to the 54th New York, the position as indicated by the monument and markers seems small for the estimated size of this regiment. There is no documentary evidence from the regiment itself, but the Bachelder map confirms the position at the wall beside Brickyard Lane. As mentioned above, statements from Lt. Whittier of the 5th Maine and Lt. Miller of the 153rd Pennsylvania appear to confirm this position. However, Lt. W. Beidelman, also a member of Miller's regiment, claimed the 68th N.Y. was the regiment whose line was refused to the north (see also 153rd PA).

153rd Pennsylvania [*~342 members / 130 ft.—no flank markers*] The position for this regiment is something of an enigma. Marked by a tablet in the next field south of the 68th New York, this placement of the 153rd Pennsylvania is consistent with Bachelder's map, although the allotted space is far too small. Other evidence places the regiment in this position at some point, but earlier on July 2. In a somewhat muddled 1886 letter to Col. Bachelder, Lt. J. C. Miller describes returning to this position at sunset, finding that the regiment had moved "up towards town and...between the two stone walls." Col. von Gilsa was, "standing to the rear of where our tablet was erected," and directed Miller and his men "down towards the wall towards the left [north] from where we were standing." In an 1887 letter to Bachelder, Lt. W. Beidelman agrees, stating emphatically that the unit's marker should be in the next field to the north—but added that the regiment, "never was in that field where the stone is placed."

Although seemingly detailed, Lt. Miller's post-war statements are the source of much of the confusion surrounding this section of the Federal position. In his letter to Bachelder, Lt. Miller describes going to the spring in front of the 54th and 68th New York after the attack, but he later states that, "the 54th and 68th were on our right on the morning of the 3d." If Miller's statements are accurate (and after 23 years this is suspect) only a few realistic scenarios are possible: (1) Miller's regiment was really to the left of the New Yorkers' position just above the small spring by the 17th Connecticut; (2) the 54th and 68th New York were posted by Menchey's Spring during the attack—both of which seem unlikely in the face of other evidence; or, (3) with the arrival of Carroll's Brigade, the two New York regiments were moved to the right of the 153rd Pennsylvania where Miller saw them on July 3.

View to the north up Wainright Avenue from the right flank marker for the 33rd Massachusetts. The 41st New York monument is visible on the left over 400 feet away.

41st New York [*145 members / 116 ft.—The 41st arrived after the battle on July 1, and probably had more men in the ranks than this estimate suggests.*] This position is marked today with a monument and flank markers just south of the 153rd Pennsylvania, but the Bachelder map for July 2 suggests this regiment was in the next field south (facing Menchey's Spring). The position as marked does seem small for a regiment of this size, but it seems likely that at least the left of the regiment's line was at the wall here. In a version of Lt. Miller's account (see 153rd PA) printed in the regimental history, he describes retreating to the lane and finding the 41st New York in this position just previous to the attack. Lt. Col. von Einsiedel's seemingly detailed report for the regiment is of little help here, for he confuses the positions of July 2 and 3, i.e., Carroll's regiments are on his left, in addition to the 153rd PA, and the 54th and 68th New York.

Detached from Smith's Brigade (2nd Brig., 2nd Div., 11th Corps)
33rd Massachusetts [*461 members / 211 ft.*] The position of the regiment is marked today with its left flank at the wall just north of Slocum Avenue and its right at the wall behind the McKnight house—a very small space for what was probably the largest regiment in this area. Odd also is the gap along the wall between the left of this regiment and the right of the 41st New York some 150 yards to the northwest. (Located some 60 yards up the hill from the right flank of the 41st New York is what appears to be the wrought iron stem for an early plaque. The base is identical to that on other early Massachusetts markers, but the writer has been unable to determine its original purpose).

In his report on the attack, Col. Underwood stated only that the regiment was, "in the valley, behind a wall in part occupied by a New York regiment of the 1st division." After taking an active part in repulsing the attack, the regiment then moved "still further to the right along a wall in front of an orchard, to the immediate right of Steven's Maine battery." Strangely, it is this second position that appears on Bachelder's map, placing the Bay State regiment entirely on the McKnight lot. (It should be noted here that the course of part of the wall south of the intersection was shifted somewhat during the construction of Slocum Avenue). If Underwood's description of the regiment's part in the repulse of the Confederate attack is accurate, both the markers and Bachelder's placement seem too far to the right.

Summary

The placement of the markers for Harris' Brigade appears to be fairly consistent with other available information on their position. There is little doubt the markers are intended to reflect the position of the regiments on the evening of July 2 (i.e., the 25th Ohio is on the hillside and the 17th Connecticut is along the lane—see Map 8). Bachelder's placement of the 107th and 25th Ohio stretches virtually from the Baltimore Pike to Brickyard Lane, and the 17th Connecticut barely covers the gap on the brigade's right—a thin line indeed.

The placement of Von Gilsa's regiments is more of a puzzle. Although available evidence more or less confirms the arrangement of memorials along Wainwright Avenue, it is unlikely these markers represent the exact placement of the regiments on the evening of July 2. But it also seems unlikely that the GBMA (or the veterans themselves) would intentionally place the monuments entirely out of context with the action. One likely scenario—a consensus of sorts—places these regiments as follows (starting to the right of the 17th Connecticut on Map 8):

With only contradictory information available, the arrangement of the New York regiments on von Gilsa's left seems to be the most in doubt. Strangely, the evidence indicates one New York regiment (probably the 54th) was placed at a right angle to the lane, while the other (probably the 68th) occupied the left of the brigade line next to the 17th Connecticut. If so, the regiments' memorials might represent a position held earlier on July 2. Perhaps when Miller's 153rd Pennsylvania "closed up towards the town," the New Yorkers also shifted up the lane; with the arrival of the larger Connecticut regiment, one of the regiments was placed in reserve.

Despite other differences in their statements, both Lt. Miller and Lt. Beidleman appear to place the 153rd Pennsylvania in the field below Ricketts' Battery, probably following a northward shift in the brigade line. The regiment's placement on the Bachelder map and the position of their tablet probably reflect the earlier position described by Miller.

The monument for the 41st New York appears to be a fairly good indicator of where the regiment stood during the attack (and is about where Lt. Miller describes finding their line). Given the estimated size of the regiment, however, their line probably extended further toward Menchey's Spring (closer to the area where Bachelder places them).

There seems little doubt that the 33rd Massachusetts occupied a position about where their memorial is located. But it is improbable that Col. Underwood would position his regiment with a 150 yard gap to their left. If Underwood started his line to the right of the 41st New York north of Menchey's Spring, a two ranked formation of this regiment would still reach the wall on the McKnight property; given Underwood's statements and the space available, this position seems to make more sense.

Base of an early plaque located near Wainwright Avenue. Although similar to early Massachusetts markers, the original inscription is unknown. Stevens' Knoll and the 33rd Massachusetts monument are visible in the distance.

ENDNOTES

Preface

1. Harlan D. Unrau, *Administrative History of Gettysburg National Military Park and Cemetery*, United States Dept. of Interior/National Park Service, July 1991, 5.

July 1

1. U.S. War Department, *The War of the Rebellion: A Compilation of the Official Records of the Union and Confederate Armies*, 70 vols. in 128 parts (Washington, D.C.: Government Printing Office, 1880-1901), Series 1, vol. 27, Part 1,702. Hereafter referred to as "*OR*, Part__, p.__." Unless noted, all references are from Series 1, Vol. 27.

2. David L. & Audrey J. Ladd, eds., *The Bachelder Papers—Gettysburg in Their Own Words*, 3 vols. New Hampshire Historical Society, Reprint. (Dayton, OH: Morningside Press), 1994, vol. 2, 1182. Hereafter referred to as *BP*; N.Y. Monuments Commission for the Battlefields of Gettysburg and Chattanooga, *Final Report of the Battlefield of Gettysburg*, 3 vols. (Albany: J. B. Lyon & Co., 1900), vol. 3, 721. Hereafter referred to as *NY at Gettysburg*.

3. *OR*, Part 1, 721.

4. *OR*, Part 1, 704.

5. Allan Nevins, ed., *A Diary of Battle: The Personal Journals of Col. Charles S. Wainwright* (New York: Harcourt, Brace & World), 1962, 237; *OR*, Part 1, 704-5.

6. *OR*, Part 1, 717-8.

7. Jacob Smith, *Camps and Campaigns of the 107th Regiment Ohio Volunteer Infantry Aug. 1862-July 1865* (np. nd.), 88.

8. *BP*, vol. 1, 312, 748; Kenneth Bandy & Florence Freeland, *The Gettysburg Papers*, 3 vols. (Dayton, Ohio: Morningside Press, 1978) vol. 1, 259. Col. Meyer, who was ill according to some accounts, was relieved of command on July 1 for "incapacity and cowardice" according to Captain Young.

9. *BP*, vol. 3, 1350; Letter of General Winfield Scott Hancock, *Southern Historical Society Papers*, vol. 5. (1878),169.

10. *OR*, Part 1, 704.

11. *Gettysburg Papers*, vol. 2, 760.

12. *OR*, Part 2, 484; John Busey & David Martin, *Regimental Strengths and Losses at Gettysburg* (Hightstown, N.J.: Longstreet House, 1986), 286; *BP*, vol. 3, 1350. Brig. Gen. R. F. Hoke was recovering from wounds received at Chancellorsville two months before. The last regiment of the

brigade, the 54th North Carolina, was on detached duty and did not rejoin the brigade until after the battle.

13. Charles Hamlin, et al, *Maine at Gettysburg* (Portland: Lakeside Press, 1898), 89; *OR*, Part 2, 484.

14. *Regimental Strengths and Losses*, 286; Letter of Joseph W. Jackson, 8th Louisiana Vertical File, GNMP Library. In 1861, the original "Tigers" were actually a single New Orleans company of dubious reputation belonging to Chatham Wheat's 1st Louisiana Battalion. At some point, Wheat's whole unit seems to have acquired the nickname. When the battalion was absorbed by other Louisiana regiments after Wheat's death in 1862, the entire brigade would take on the battalion's name and reputation for hard fighting.

15. Mark Dunkleman and Michael Winey, "The Hardtack Regiment in the Brickyard Fight" *Gettysburg Magazine* (January, 1993), 23. Despite the ongoing debate, we should remember that had Ewell been able to reorganize in time for an attack on July 1—a dubious proposition in itself—he would have encountered the same problems he faced the following evening: lack of support and a Federal position lined with artillery.

16. *Regimental Strengths and Losses*, 253; *BP*, vol. 1, 743; William H. Warren, *History of the Seventeenth Connecticut 1862-1865* (np., copy courtesy Bridgeport Historical Society); Letter of A.W. Peck, 591.

17. *Gettysburg Papers*, Account of Rufus Dawes, vol. 1, 383-4.

July 2: A.M.

1. *Camps and Campaigns of the 107th Ohio*, 93.

2. *History of the 17th Connecticut*, Letter of W.W. Paynton, 592.

3. *Ibid.*, 625-6.

4. *BP*, vol. 2, 1212.

5. *NY at Gettysburg*, vol. 3, 1247.

6. Letter of Lt. Edward Whittier, 5th Maine Battery Vertical File, GNMP Library.

7. *History of the 17th Connecticut*, Letter of W.W. Paynton, 593; *OR*, Part 1, 718.

8. *Regimental Strengths and Losses*, 253; Letter of Col. A. B. Underwood, National Archives, Copy on file GNMP Library.

9. *BP*, vol. 2, 1212.

10. J. W. Jackson letter.

11. *BP*, vol. 1, 460. Historian J.B. Bachelder's map for July 2 shows Hays' regiments arranged along the stream in the same order as their advance on July 1, with the 5th Louisiana near Baltimore Street, with the 6th, 9th, 7th and 8th Louisiana in line to the east. Another version of Bachelder's map shows one of the Louisiana regiments positioned behind the main line; given the amount of space along Winebrenner's Run for a brigade

of this size, the latter arrangement makes more sense. General Hays does not specifically mention the brigade's arrangement on July 2.

12. Journal of Capt. William Seymour, copy on file GNMP Library.
13. Edward Marcus, ed., *A New Canaan Private in the Civil War; The Letters of Justus M. Silliman* (New Canaan, CT: New Canaan Historical Society, 1884) letter dated 7/3/63; *History of the 17th Connecticut*, 690.
14. William R. Kiefer, *History of the One Hundred Fifty-Third Regiment Pennsylvania Volunteer Infantry* (Easton, PA: Chemical Publishing, 1909), 221.
15. Wayne Andrews, ed., *Autobiography of Carl Schurz* (New York: Charles Scribner's Sons, 1961), 266-7; *OR*, Part 2, 446.

Benner's Hill

1. *OR*, Part 2, 446-7; Jay Jorgensen "Joseph W. Latimer, the 'Boy Major' at Gettysburg" *Gettysburg Magazine*, (January, 1994), 30-1.
2. John Nicholson, ed., *Pennsylvania at Gettysburg: Ceremonies at the Dedication of the Monuments Erected by the Commonwealth of Pennsylvania*, 2 vols. (Harrisburg: W. Stanley Ray, State Printer, 1904), 881; *A New Canaan Private*, 42.
3. *Wainwright Journal*, 243; *Pennsylvania at Gettysburg*, 881; *BP*, vol. 1, 32.
4. *Wainwright Journal*, 243-4.
5. A. B. Underwood letter; *Wainwright Journal*, 243.
6. *History of the 17th Connecticut*, 593-4.
7. *Maine at Gettysburg*, 93; L. Van Loan Naisawald, *Grape and Canister* (New York: Oxford Univ. Press, 1960), 402; *OR*, Part 2, 544.
8. Harry Pfanz, *Gettysburg: Culp's Hill and Cemetery Hill* (Chapel Hill: Univ. of N.C. Press, 1993), 187.
9. Text of Latimer's Monuments, Benner's Hill, GNMP; *Gettysburg Papers*, vol. 2, 329; *OR*, Part 1, 894; *BP*, vol. 1, 745.

Early's Advance

1. *OR*, Part 2, 556.
2. Seymour Journal; *OR*, Part 2, 480; *A New Canaan Private*, 42.
3. Walter Clark, ed., *Histories of the Several Regiments and Battalions From North Carolina in the Great War, 1861-1865*, 5 vols. (Raleigh: State of North Carolina, 1901), vol. 1, 331, Hereafter referred to as *North Carolina in the War*; *Ibid.*, vol. 2, 136.
4. *Ibid.*, vol. 3, 415; J.W. Jackson letter.
5. *Maine at Gettysburg*, 94-5; *Gettysburg Papers*, vol. 2, 773.
6. *History of the 153rd Pennsylvania*, 219-20.
7. Seymour Journal.
8. *BP*, vol. 2, 212.

9. *North Carolina in the War*, vol. 1, 313.
10. *OR*, Part 2, 484.
11. *Maine at Gettysburg*, 95. Although Lt. Whittier's account here appears to describe the advance as a single line, most accounts describe two or three lines. See also Harry Pfanz's, *Culp's Hill & Cemetery Hill*.
12. *North Carolina in the War*, vol. 3, 416; Memoirs of Pvt. Thomas Causby, 6th North Carolina, Brake Collection, USAMHI, Carlisle, Pa. Col. Archibald Godwin, who succeeded Avery, would not learn of his death until after the attack.
13. *OR*, Part 1, 894; *Wainwright Journal*, 245; *Pennsylvania at Gettysburg*, 882; *BP*, vol. 1, 237. In another ongoing dispute, Ricketts claimed to have moved into Cooper's position long before 7:00 p.m. Wainwright's account clearly places Cooper on the hill until "about sundown."
14. *OR*, Part 1, 714; A. B. Underwood letter; *BP*, vol. 1, 745.

Brickyard Lane

1. Map of the Battlefield at Gettysburg (Gettysburg: Gettysburg National Park Commission, 1901). This map, known as the "Cope map" for Colonel E. Cope (Park engineer from 1893 to 1922), shows the battlefield at the turn of the century. A second Cope map depicts the field as it was believed to be at the time of the battle.
2. *OR*, Part 1, 718.
3. *History of the 17th Connecticut*, Letter of M. Daniel, 561-2.
4. It appears the Park commissioners at the turn of the century felt it more expedient for Wainwright Avenue to cut across the nose of the hill. It was not unusual for construction crews of that time to use readily available materials, i.e., historic stone walls and nearby earth, to construct the present roadways. See Thomas A. Desjardin, *Stand Firm ye Boys from Maine* (Gettysburg, Pa: Thomas Publications, 1995) for a detailed discussion of this practice.
5. *BP*, vol. 2, 1213; *History of the 153rd Pennsylvania*, 141. Lt. Miller's account indicates von Gilsa stood just to the rear of where the regiment's marker was placed. Their new position would then be in the field below Ricketts' Battery.
6. *History of the 17th Connecticut*, 595.
7. *Ibid.*, Letter of W. W. Paynton, 632.
8. The monument for the 17th Connecticut apparently reflects the regiment's position after their shift; we can assume that the Ohio markers also represent the positions of these regiments at that time.
9. *BP*, vol. 2, 745-6.
10. *OR*, Part 1, 718; Seymour Journal.
11. *BP*, vol. 2, 746; *Ibid.*, vol. 3, Letter of A. Rider, 1118; *Campaigns of the 107th Ohio*, 101. Although not mentioned in any accounts, contem-

porary photographs, as well as the later Cope maps, indicate the eastern slope in front of the Ohio regiments was covered with low cornstalks.

12. Edward Culp, *The 25th Ohio Infantry in the War for the Union* (Topeka, Kansas: Geo. Crane Publ., 1885), 78-80; *BP*, vol. 2, 745-6; *OR*, Part 1, 717; *Ibid.*, Part 2, 480.

13. Carl M. Becker and Ritchie Thomas, eds., *Hearth and Knapsack: The Ladley Letters 1857-1880* (Athens, Ohio: Ohio University Press).

14. Unidentified letter, 75th Ohio Vertical File, GNMP Library. The writer has found no further mention of the capture of this flag. See Note #85.

15. *History of the 17th Connecticut*, 562-3; *Ibid.*, 717.

16. Available descriptions of the regimental positions in this area are confusing at best. See the accounts of: Col. von Einsiedel, 41st N.Y., *OR*, Part 1, 714; Lt. E. Whittier, *Gettysburg Papers*, vol. 2, 771; Lt. J. C. Miller, 153rd Pennsylvania, *BP*, vol. 2, 1213; Lt. W. Beidelman, 153rd Pennsylvania, *BP*, vol. 3, 1488-9.

17. *BP*, vol. 2, 1213; *History of the 153rd Pennsylvania*, 141-2.

18. *New York at Gettysburg*, vol. 1, 404.

19. Letter of L.E.C. Moore, "Charge of the Louisianians," *National Tribune* (August 5, 1909); *BP*, vol. 1, 245.

20. *Wainwright Journal*, 245; *History of the 17th Connecticut*, 562.

Breakthrough

1. *OR*, Part 2, 484.

2. *Maine at Gettysburg*, 95; *OR*, Part 2, 480; Causby Memoirs.

3. *North Carolina in the War*, vol. 2, 136.

4. *OR*, Part 2, 484; *North Carolina in the War*, vol. 3, 415.

5. *Maine at Gettysburg*, 96-7; *Gettysburg Papers*, vol. 2, 775.

6. A. B. Underwood letter.

7. *OR*, Part 1, 714; David Martin, *Carl Bournemann's Regiment—the 41st New York Infantry* (Hightstown, NJ: Longstreet House, 1987), 154.

8. *OR*, Part 2, 484; Richard W. Iobst, *The Bloody Sixth: The Sixth North Carolina Regiment* (Durham, N.C.: Christian Printing, 1965),137 footnote.

9. *North Carolina in the War*, vol. 2, 137.

The Struggle for the Crest

1. J. W. Jackson letter; *BP*, vol. 1, 311. Connecticut Lieutenant A. W. Peck later recalled "seeing a rebel color bearer lying dead near our batteries [the] next morning. I also saw a large dead reb who had a straw hat on; his sleeves were rolled up. He had no coat on, he wore a U.S. belt with the U.S. plate turned upside down. I picked up a couple of stars that had been torn from a rebel flag and a piece of flag also." There is no way to know if Peck found part of the flag seized by Captain Young or

that torn up by members of the 75th Ohio. No trace of either banner survives today.

2. *OR*, Part 1, 894; Letter of Lt. Charles B. Brockway, 1st Pennsylvania Artillery File, GNMP Library; Letter of William H. Thurston, "A Ricketts Batteryman Supports Carroll" *National Tribune* (October 13, 1892),4; *BP*, vol. 1, 237. The lunettes we see on East Cemetery Hill today are the result of restorations performed in the years after the battle. However, there appear to be differences in the location of some of the present works, and those indicated on early photographs and surveys of the hill. For a detailed discussion of the problem, see William A. Frassanito's *Early Photography at Gettysburg* (Gettysburg, PA: Thomas Publications, 1995), 142-6.

3. *OR*, Part 2, 486.

4. C. Brockway letter.

5. *OR*, Part 2, 489; Seymour Journal.

6. *OR*, Part 2, 556.

7. *Ibid.*, See also accounts of B. Ross & J. Huffman, Ramseur's Brigade, Brake Collection, USAMHI, Carlisle, Pa.

8. Jubal A. Early, "Leading Confederates on the Battlefield," *SHSP*, Vol. 4 (1877), 280-1.

The Repulse

1. *OR*, Part 1, 730-1; A. F. Sweetland "Repulsing the 'Tigers' at the Cemetery," *National Tribune* (Dec. 12, 1909); Text of Coster's Brigade monuments, East Cemetery Hill, GNMP. There is little information on the movements of Coster's regiments. The marker for the 73rd Pennsylvania describes moving "hastily" from Evergreen Cemetery to meet the attack on July 2, but the monument and flank markers for the 27th Pennsylvania seem to indicate the regiment was posted at the wall north of Wiedrich's battery on the previous evening .

2. *OR*, Part 1, 457; Letter of Charles Myerhoff, "What Troops Did Carroll's Brigade Displace" *National Tribune* (April 24, 1890).

3. *Ibid.*; Letter of E. H. C. Caines "A Gettysburg Diary," *National Tribune* (December 23, 1909); William Kepler, *A History of...the Fourth Ohio Volunteer Infantry in the War for the Union* (Cleveland: Leader Printing, 1886),130. Interestingly enough, if the flank markers for the 4th Ohio are accurate, the regiment would have faced down the Baltimore Pike at some point.

4. *OR*, Part 2, 480-1.

5. Thomas Elmore "Torrid Heat and Blinding Rain: A Meteorological and Astronomical Chronology of the Gettysburg Campaign," *Gettysburg Magazine*, (July, 1995), 18; *OR*, Part 2, 486; *North Carolina in the War*, vol. 1, 313.

6. *North Carolina in the War*, vol. 2, 138.
7. *OR*, Part 1, 457-9.
8. Seymour Journal; Diary of Sgt. B. Y. Malone, 6th North Carolina, Brake Collection, USAMHI, Carlisle, Pa.
9. *A New Canaan Private*, 42; *OR*, Part 2, 481, 485.
10. *NY at Gettysburg*, vol. 2, 664; *OR*, Part 1, 457-9, 718-9; *BP*, vol. 1, 139; *Ibid.*, vol. 2, 747.

Epilogue
1. Seymour Journal.
2. For a detailed discussion of the controversy surrounding this action, see Gary Lash, *The Gibraltar Brigade on East Cemetery Hill.*
3. *Regimental Strengths and Losses*, 286.
4. *Ibid.*, 253.
5. John Bachelder, *Gettysburg: What to See, How to See It* (Boston: J.B. Bachelder, 1873) 42.

INDEX

THOMAS PUBLICATIONS publishes books about the American Colonial era, the Revolutionary War, the Civil War, and other important topics. For a complete list of titles, please write to:

THOMAS PUBLICATIONS
P.O. Box 3031
Gettysburg, PA 17325